DAY HIKING THE
DANIEL BOONE NATIONAL FOREST

Other University of Tennessee Press books by Johnny Molloy

Trial by Trail: Backpacking in the Smokies, new updated edition

*Mount Rogers National Recreation Area Guidebook:
A Complete Resource for Outdoor Enthusiasts,* 3rd edition

Day Hiking the Daniel Boone National Forest

Includes Natural Bridge and Cumberland Falls State Parks

JOHNNY MOLLOY

The University of Tennessee Press / Knoxville

Copyright © 2019 by The University of Tennessee Press / Knoxville.
All Rights Reserved. Manufactured in the United States of America.
First Edition.

Digital topographic maps used by permission of Garmin Ltd. All rights reserved.

Disclaimer: This book is meant only as a guide to hikes in the greater Daniel Boone National Forest area and does not guarantee hiker safety in any way. Hike at your own risk. Neither the University of Tennessee Press nor Johnny Molloy is liable for property loss or damage, personal injury, or death that may result from accessing or hiking the trails described in this guide.

LIBRARY OF CONGRESS CATALOGING-IN-PUBLICATION DATA
Names: Molloy, Johnny, 1961– author.
Title: Day hiking the Daniel Boone National Forest: includes Natural Bridge and Cumberland Falls State Parks / Johnny Molloy.
Description: First Edition. | Knoxville, Tennessee: The University of Tennessee Press, [2019] | Includes index. | Identifiers: LCCN 2018029989 (print) | LCCN 2018057653 (ebook) | ISBN 9781621904953 (Kindle) | ISBN 9781621904960 (pdf) |
ISBN 9781621904946 | ISBN 9781621904946 (paperback)
Subjects: LCSH: Hiking—Kentucky—Daniel Boone National Forest—Guidebooks. | Daniel Boone National Forest (Ky.)—Guidebooks.
Classification: LCC GV199.42.K4 (ebook) | LCC GV199.42.K4 M65 2019 (print) | DDC 796.5209769—dc23
LC record available at https://lccn.loc.gov/2018029989

To all the trail builders and hikers
who wander the trails of Kentucky

Contents

Preface --- xiii
Introduction -------------------------------------- xvii
Hiking Summary Guide ------------------------------ xxii
Suggested Hikes ----------------------------------- xxvii

RED RIVER GORGE AND CAVE RUN LAKE AREA

Furnace Arch --- 1
Double Arch -- 5
Courthouse Rock Loop --------------------------------- 9
Grays Arch D Boon Hut ------------------------------- 13
Chimney Top Creek Hike ------------------------------ 17
Princess Arch Chimney Top Rock ---------------------- 21
Indian Arch --- 25
Clifty Wilderness Loop ------------------------------ 28
Angel Windows Whistling Arch Sky Bridge ------------- 32
Rock Bridge Arch Creation Falls Turtle Falls -------- 36
Hidden Arch Silvermine Arch ------------------------- 41
Whittleton Arch ------------------------------------- 45
Natural Bridge Loop --------------------------------- 49
Sand Gap Loop --------------------------------------- 53

CENTRAL DANIEL BOONE NATIONAL FOREST

Alcorn Branch Falls --------------------------------- 59
Turkey Foot Loop ------------------------------------ 63
Resurgence Cave ------------------------------------- 67
Hawk Creek Suspension Bridge and Falls -------------- 71

SOUTHERN DANIEL BOONE NATIONAL FOREST

Rockcastle Narrows East Loop ------------------------ 77
Cane Creek via Bald Rock Picnic Area ---------------- 81
Bee Rock Loop --------------------------------------- 85
Falls of Pounder Branch and Vanhook Falls ----------- 89

Laurel River Lake Loop	93
Flatwoods Trail	97
The Scuttle Hole	100
Lakeside South Loop	104
Beaver Creek Wilderness Loop	108
Bark Camp Creek Cascades and Shelter	112
Dog Slaughter Falls Star Creek Falls and Shelter	118
Cumberland Falls Dog Slaughter Falls	122
Eagle Falls Cumberland Falls	127
Blue Bend Loop	131
Natural Arch Scenic Area and Loop	135
North Fork Big Creek Falls	139
Barren Fork Heritage Trail	143
Yahoo Falls Yahoo Arch	147
Markers Arch Yahoo Arch	151
Lick Creek Falls Princess Falls	154
Marks Branch Falls Gobblers Arch Loop	159
Buffalo Arch	163

Illustrations

FIGURES

Author Stands Below Furnace Arch	2
Morning Light Through Double Arch	7
Courthouse Rock Loop	9
Red River Gorge	14
Kentucky's Fabled Red River	18
Chimney Top Rock	23
Historic Gladie Cabin	26
Clifty Wilderness Loop	30
A Pair of Young Hikers	34
Creation Falls	38
Seventy-eight Wooden Steps	42
Whittleton Arch	47
Lovers Leap	50
Fat Mans Squeeze	54
Alcorn Branch Falls	60
Turkey Foot Recreation Area	64
War Fork Resurges from Resurgence Cave	69
Suspension Bridge Falls	72
Vanhook Falls	79
Trail Bridges	82
Bee Rock	86
Cataract 1.5 Miles into Hike	91
Trails Alongside Laurel River Lake	94
View of Laurel River Lake	98
Rockcastle River Arm	102
Wildflowers	106
Beaver Creek Wilderness	110
Bark Camp Creek Cascades	114
Dog Slaughter Falls	120
Cumberland Falls	125
Eagle Falls	128
Circuit Hike	133
Natural Arch	137

North Fork Big Creek Falls 141
Barren Fork's Coal Mining Heritage 143
Yahoo Falls 149
Markers Arch 153
Princess Falls 156
Marks Branch Falls 160
Buffalo Arch 165

MAPS

Furnace Arch 3
Double Arch 6
Courthouse Rock Loop 10
Grays Arch D Boon Hut 15
Chimney Top Creek Hike 19
Princess Arch Chimney Top Rock 22
Indian Arch 27
Clifty Wilderness Hike 29
Angel Windows Whistling Arch Sky Bridge 33
Rock Bridge Arch Creation Falls Turtle Falls 37
Hidden Arch Silvermine Arch 43
Whittleton Arch 46
Natural Bridge Loop 51
Sand Gap Loop 55
Alcorn Branch Falls 61
Turkey Foot Loop 65
Resurgence Cave 68
Hawk Creek Suspension Bridge and Falls 73
Rockcastle Narrows East Loop 78
Cane Creek via Bald Rock Picnic Area 83
Bee Rock Loop 87
Falls of Pounder Branch and Vanhook Falls 90
Laurel River Lake Loop 95
Flatwoods Trail 99
The Scuttle Hole 101
Lakeside South Loop 105
Beaver Creek Wilderness Loop 109
Bark Camp Creek Cascades 113
Bark Camp Creek Cascades and Shelter 116
Dog Slaughter Falls Star Creek Falls and Shelter 119

Cumberland Falls Dog Slaughter Falls	123
Cumberland Falls Dog Slaughter Falls	124
Eagle Falls Cumberland Falls	129
Blue Bend Loop	132
Natural Arch Scenic Area and Loop	136
North Fork Big Creek Falls	140
Barren Fork Heritage Trail	144
Yahoo Falls Yahoo Arch	148
Markers Arch Yahoo Arch	152
Lick Creek Falls Princess Falls	155
Marks Branch Falls Gobblers Arch Loop	161
Buffalo Arch	164

Preface

When thinking of Kentucky, I recall its vast natural resources, from the bluffs above the Mississippi River to Mammoth Cave National Park, the lakes of the central state to the mountains, hills and hollows of the east. Others may see the state through a different lens, but I love Kentucky for its great outdoors and the opportunities that it presents.

And Kentucky's Daniel Boone National Forest (DBNF) offers what I think is the crown jewel of the Bluegrass State's outdoor attractions. My first taste of the DBNF was hiking trails adjacent to the Big South Fork National Recreation Area, on the border of Kentucky and Tennessee. I saw that trails in the Big South Fork connected with trails of the DBNF and naturally extended my hiking and backpacking adventures into the DBNF. And I enjoyed the features of this big land—sheer bluffs, arches, delicate veil-like waterfalls, cabin-sized boulders, rock shelters and powerful whitewater rivers.

In the course of attempting to hike every trail at the Big South Fork I encountered the Sheltowee Trace, Kentucky's north-south master path running 300 miles through the length of the Daniel Boone National Forest. Time passed and I became an outdoor writer, hiking, paddling and camping for a living. The Sheltowee Trace began popping up all over the place as I researched and wrote Best Tent Camping: Kentucky. The first place I saw it again was at Clear Creek Lake Campground, in northern Kentucky, near the town of Morehead. From the campground, I walked the Sheltowee Trace on a long narrow ridge that looked down on Clear Creek Lake and led to Furnace Arch. Not only did the arch itself hold appeal but the vista from atop it extended for untold miles that clear day.

Later, I stayed at Turkey Foot Campground, a great destination in its own right. Once again, the Sheltowee Trace offered a chance to explore the surroundings. I took the path north from Turkey Foot through the War Fork gorge to reach Resurgence Cave, where War Fork emerges after running underground for some distance. Not only did cool water flow from Resurgence Cave, but an eerie mist hovered around its opening on that warm rainy afternoon. The Sheltowee Trace ran through Koomer Ridge Campground, and into and through the famed Red River Gorge, where I explored Chimney Top Creek and walked across the swinging bridge over the Red River.

After hiking the Sheltowee Trace through the Red River Gorge, I determined to thru-hike and write a guide for Sheltowee Trace, capturing the essence of this 319-mile path, in its deep hemlock woods, its oak forests and its rock rims where waterfalls drop and mountain vistas fade in the distance.

While undertaking the Sheltowee Trace project I walked from one end of the DBNF to another. Seeing the beauty along the Sheltowee Trace made me want to explore the national forest beyond the Sheltowee Trace. More than a decade after penning the Sheltowee Trace guide I decided to write this book, covering the best day hikes within the DBNF, drawing not only from the Sheltowee Trace but also all the trails within the entire DBNF trail inventory.

Just like life at home, life on the trail wasn't always great, like the ultimate case of chiggers ever gotten by mankind, being barraged by windblown snow on a long tent-less night, or fighting through a trailless segment of the Beaver Creek Wilderness. However, these experiences were spices in the entrée. I also saw the lush Hawk Creek valley from a suspension bridge, the Red River Gorge bathed in fall colors, and the span of Natural Arch above magical woodland.

I hope this guide leads you on as many enjoyable adventures as I have had in the DBNF, from the trails of Cave Run Lake up near Morehead to the backcountry of Marks Branch down Whitley City way. I have encountered abundant natural splendor while working on this book. Certain scenes immediately come to mind—the wide wall of white that is Princess Falls, the winding wooded shoreline of Laurel River Lake and coursing Swift Camp Run Creek. I recall walking through the view-laden sandstone on Auxier Ridge, cutting through the Scuttle Hole and stepping down the incredible wooden stairway en route to Silvermine Arch.

I can hear the Cumberland River roar through its famed falls and downstream rapids. I can feel the chill morning air while looping through Clifty Wilderness. I can sense the overhang above me while heading up to Bee Rock. I can feel the thick humidity while walking along the Rockcastle River. I recollect a menagerie of superlative scenery that can be found along the hiking trails of the Daniel Boone National Forest.

And what a treat it was to absorb the best scenes along the best hikes that together paint a mosaic of ecosystems within the Daniel Boone National Forest! I took the duty very seriously, drawing upon my years of experience our country while authoring more than 60 outdoor guides throughout the United States, including several specific to Kentucky. I wanted to get it right. To this end, I included hikes that paint an accurate picture of what the Daniel Boone National Forest has to offer. May you will find the hikes contained as rewarding as I have.

Throughout the process, I kept looking for the best of the best and found some new sights—panoramas of the Red River Gorge from atop Double Arch, the dashing cascade above Turkey Foot Campground, and the trail stairs and rockhouse along Lick Creek. After completing the task of writing this book, I came away with an even more profound respect for the Daniel Boone National Forest. I hope you will, too. Happy hiking!

Thanks to the personnel of the Daniel Boone National Forest, Cumberland Falls State Park, Natural Bridge State Park, and all those who walk the trails of this heavenly slice of the Bluegrass State. And thanks most of all to my wife Keri Anne.

Introduction

This guide details 40 hikes in Kentucky's Daniel Boone National Forest, with the addition of hikes in two Kentucky state parks—Natural Bridge and Cumberland Falls, whose lands are enveloped by the Daniel Boone National Forest. While hiking in the DBNF, hikers will see the best of the Cumberland Plateau, from exquisite aches to bluffs that offer extensive vistas to waterfalls that descend into sandstone cathedrals.

The paths tread through deep forests in gorges cut by creeks and rivers and atop the Cumberland Plateau, where oak and pine forests range long distances. Rockhouses, caves and other geological features stand out in these rich woodlands. Did you know Kentucky has more natural arches than any state in the East?

The Daniel Boone National Forest, originally named the Cumberland National Forest, was established in the 1930s. It covers over 700,000 acres in parts of 21 counties in eastern Kentucky. Before the establishment of the national forest, uncontrolled logging and mining had ravaged the land. The forest has since recovered nicely. Later, other areas were set aside purely for their natural beauty, such as Cumberland Falls State Park, Natural Bridge State Park, the Clifty Wilderness, and Red River Gorge Geological Area.

With the protection of these areas has come protection of the plants and animals that live here, including threatened and endangered species such as the red-cockaded woodpecker, Virginia big-eared bat, freshwater mussels, and white-haired goldenrod. The black bear has made a comeback in these parts, expanding its range into eastern Kentucky from neighboring states.

Hikes in this guidebook range in distance, difficulty and destination, to offer the breadth of hiking experiences to be had within the DBNF. The shortest hike is under a mile, with the longest being 10 miles, with most of them somewhere in the middle. Most hikes are loops where possible, though by necessity some are there-and-back endeavors. Parts of some hikes cover paved paths while others traverse rugged, rocky irregular terrain, or a mix of both. Hike highlights visit waterfalls, arches, overlooks and geologically fascinating valleys.

Hikes include a loop through the Beaver Creek Wilderness, a visit to Marks Branch Falls and Gobblers Arch, a traverse through the gorge of the mighty Cumberland River, a walk to Eagle Falls and Cumberland Falls at Cumberland Falls State Park. Another hike heads down the most beautiful of creek valleys to Bark Camp Cascades. Still another leads you down Hawk Creek to a suspension bridge and waterfall. And there's the hike to Indian Arch followed by a short climb and incredible view from atop the stone span. The walk to Sky Bridge is great for the family, especially when you add a meal at the nearby picnic area.

Peruse the book or check the hikes chart at the guide's beginning, and you will certainly find a hike in the Daniel Boone National Forest that will fit your desires. I hope this guide helps you to appreciate and enjoy the Kentucky national treasure that is the Daniel Boone National Forest.

HOW TO USE THIS GUIDE

Each hike has its own unique description. A short hike summary is located at the beginning of each hike. It gives an overview of what the hike is like—the terrain, what you might see along the way, and why you should go. Following the hike summary is an information box that allows the hiker quick access to pertinent information: hike distance, time, difficulty, highlights, cautions, fees/permits, other trail users and trail contacts. Below is an example of a box included with a hike:

BUFFALO ARCH

Hike Summary: This hike takes place in the most southwesterly portion of the entire Daniel Boone National Forest. From this remote locale, pick up the Parkers Mountain Trail, tracing a ridge. Join the narrow Buffalo Arch Trail, circling the upper reaches of Right Fork Pennington Branch to reach secluded Buffalo Arch, just 1/10 mile from the Tennessee state line.

DISTANCE: 1.6-mile there-and-back
HIKING TIME: 0.9 hours
DIFFICULTY: Easy
HIGHLIGHTS: Natural arch, solitude
CAUTIONS: None
FEES/PERMITS: No fees or permits required
OTHER TRAIL USERS: None
TRAIL CONTACTS: Daniel Boone National Forest, Stearns Ranger District, 3320 US 27 North, Whitley City, KY 42653, (606)376-5323, www.fs.usda.gov/dbnf

Finding the trailhead: From the intersection of US 27 and KY 92 just south of Whitley City, take KY 92 west for 6.5 miles to turn left on KY 1363, just after bridging the Big South Fork River. Follow KY 1363 for 11 miles to a T-intersection and the end of the blacktop. Turn right onto gravel Forest Road 564. Follow FR 564 for 1.2 miles then stay right with FR 564 as FR 137 goes left. Continue on FR 564 toward Parkers Mountain for 1.5 more miles to veer left onto FR 562. Stay with FR 562 for 5.8 miles then look left for a sign and small trailhead parking area as FR 562 curves right. The parking area is small and limited. GPS Trailhead Coordinates: N36° 36.6310′, W84° 45.9990′

From the information box, we can learn the details of each particular hike. This hike is 1.6 miles long and is a there-and-back endeavor. Hiking time is the average time it will take to cover the route, and this one will take under an hour. Hiking time factors in total distance and trail conditions. Factor in your own fitness level to the given hiking time. Highlights describes the can't miss part of the trek, here the must see highlight is Buffalo Arch. Cautions reviews any potential hiking hazards, so you can be aware on the front end. Obviously, this does not cover every potential pitfall of a given hike, but does keep you apprised of any hike-specific hazards with which to contend. Fees/permits lets you know ahead of time if there is a charge to park or enter a particular place, or whether a permit is required to hike or camp. Other trail users informs as to whether the path is hiker only, or you will be sharing it with bicyclers or equestrians. Trail contacts details ways to reach the particular ranger district governing the given hike, including mailing address and phone number. Finding the trailhead gives specific directions from an easily ascertained location, usually the nearest interstate or major highway, to the hike's trailhead. GPS Trailhead Coordinates enable you to use your navigational aid to find the trailhead as well.

Following each box is a narrative of the hike. A detailed account follows, where trail junctions, stream bridges, overlooks and trailside features are noted along with their distance from the trailhead. This helps keep you apprised of your whereabouts as well as make sure you don't miss those features noted. A summary of trail mileage is given at the narrative's end, so you can quickly scan the distance to major trail intersections or highlights. All the above information should help you make the most of these Daniel Boone National Forest hikes. Now get out there and hit the trail!

WEATHER

The climate of the Daniel Boone National Forest is seasonal, with warm to hot summers and moderate winters. Early spring is the most variable, with periodic warm-ups broken by cold fronts bringing rain, then chilly temperatures. Later on, temperatures stay warm; things get downright hot by July. Typically, mornings start clear, then clouds build and hit-or-miss thunderstorms occur by afternoon. The first cool fronts hit the Daniel Boone National Forest around mid-September. Fall sees warm clear days and cool nights with the least amount of rain. Precipitation picks up in November, and temperatures generally stay cool to cold, broken by occasional mild spells. Snowfall varies winter to winter but averages less than 10 inches per year.

Below is a chart detailing the average monthly temperatures for Beattyville, Kentucky, roughly in the center of the DBNF, along with precipitation, giving you an idea of what type of weather to expect.

Month	Average High degrees	Average Low degrees	Precipitation inches
January	42	21	3.8
February	47	23	3.7
March	57	31	4.4
April	67	39	3.9
May	75	49	4.9
June	82	58	4.1
July	86	63	4.7
August	85	62	3.0
September	79	55	3.7
October	69	41	3.0
November	58	33	3.9
December	47	25	4.2

HIKING SAFETY

To some outdoor enthusiasts, the hills and hollows of the Daniel Boone National Forest seem laden with hazards—snakes, bears, wild rivers and steep cliffs. It is the fear of the unknown that causes this anxiety. No doubt, potentially dangerous situations can occur in the outdoors as well as where you live, but as long as you use sound judgment and prepare yourself before you hit the trail, you'll be much safer in the woods than most urban areas of the country. It is better to look at a hike as a fascinating discovery of the unknown, rather than a potential for disaster. Here are a few tips to make your trip safer and easier:

Always bring food and water. Food will give you energy, help keep you warm and may sustain you in an emergency until help arrives. And you never know if there will be a stream nearby when thirsty. Treat your water before drinking from a stream. The chance of getting sick from the organism known as giardia or other waterborne organism is small, but there is no reason to take a chance. Boil or filter all water before drinking it. Be prepared for mosquitoes and chiggers, with clothing and bug dope.

Stay on designated trails. Most hikers get lost when they leave the path. If you become disoriented, do not panic—that may result in a bad decision that will make your predicament worse, especially with the abundance of clifflines in the DBNF. Retrace your steps if you can remember them, or stay put. Rangers check the trails first when searching for lost or overdue hikers.

Bring a map, and lighter, and a GPS or GPS-enabled smart phone. Should you become lost, these items can help you stick around long enough to be found or get yourself out of a pickle. Trail maps are available at ranger stations, visitor centers and online. Be aware of the symptoms of hypothermia. Shivering and forgetfulness are the two most common indicators of this cold-weather killer. Hypothermia can occur when the temperature is in the 50s, especially when a wet hiker is wearing lightweight, cotton clothing. If symptoms arise, get the victim shelter, hot liquids and dry clothes or a dry sleeping bag.

Always bring rain gear. Thunderstorms can come on suddenly in the summer and winter fronts can soak you to the bone. Keep in mind that a rainy day is as much a part of nature as those idyllic ones you desire. Rainy days really cut down on the crowds. With appropriate rain gear, a normally crowded trail can be a place of solitude. Do remember that getting wet opens the door to hypothermia.

Take along your brain. A cool calculating mind is the single most important piece of equipment you'll ever need on the trail.

Think before you act. Watch your step. Plan ahead. Avoiding accidents before they happen is the best recipe for a rewarding, stress-relieving hike. Use your head out there and treat the place as if it were your own backyard.

Gather information. Before you head to your chosen destination, order a map or information kit and visit their website. This information will help you get oriented to the roads, features and attractions of your chosen hike.

Take your time along the trails. Pace yourself. Daniel Boone National Forest's wildlands are filled with wonders both big and small. We cannot always schedule our free time when we want, but try to hike during the week and to avoid the traditional holidays if possible. If you are hiking on busy days, go early in the morning, it will enhance your chances of seeing wildlife, too.

Hike	Distance (miles)	Time (hours)	Difficulty	Highlights
Furnace Arch	6.0	3.0	Moderate	Hike past views to Furnace Arch, Clear Creek iron furnace at trailhead
Double Arch	4.8	2.4	Moderate	Visit Double Arch and a sandstone knob for stellar views of the Red River Gorge.
Courthouse Rock Loop	5.1	2.7	Moderate	Enjoy multiple views of Double Arch, Haystack Rock and Courthouse Rock
Grays Arch D Boon Hut	4.7	2.3	Moderate	See geologically significant Grays Arch and historically significant D Boon Hut, views, too
Chimney Top Creek Hike	9.0	5.0	Difficult	Enjoy everywhere-you-look beauty in the Red River Gorge
Princess Arch Chimney Top Rock	1.2	.6	Easy	Soak in stellar view and arch from the same trailhead
Indian Arch	3.0	1.6	Easy	Walk to a slender sloping arch and grab a big panorama from its heights
Clifty Wilderness Hike	9.2	5.0	Difficult	Explore Clifty Wilderness on the Osborne Bend Trail in the Red River Gorge

Hike	Distance (miles)	Time (hours)	Difficulty	Highlights
Angel Windows Whistling Arch Sky Bridge	1.9	1.2	Easy	Combine three short highlight filled hikes to very different arches, views, too
Rock Bridge Arch Creation Falls Turtle Falls	4.0	2.2	Moderate	This popular hike explores an arch stretching over a creek plus two waterfalls
Hidden Arch Silvermine Arch	4.5	2.3	Easy-moderate	This two-pronged hike takes you to two separate and different arches in the Red River Gorge
Whittleton Arch	3.0	1.4	Moderate	Walk through scenic valley to reach a massive stone span
Natural Bridge Loop	3.2	1.7	Moderate	Enjoy highlights galore on one of Kentucky's best hikes
Sand Gap Loop	10.0	5.5	Difficult	This long loop explores the quiet side of Natural Bridge State Park, solitude aplenty
Alcorn Branch Falls	1.6	1.0	Easy	Visit a seldom seen part of DBNF on the Sheltowee Trace to Alcorn Branch Falls, a 30 foot seasonal spiller
Turkey Foot Loop	4.1	1.8	Easy-moderate	Cruise War Fork Valley then loop to pass a seasonal Turkey Foot Cascade
Resurgence Cave	4.8	2.3	Easy-moderate	Take the Sheltowee Trace through the War Fork valley to Resurgence Cave, a stony maw from which War Fork emerges
Hawk Creek Suspension Bridge and Falls	3.4	2.0	Moderate	Follow the Sheltowee Trace to suspension bridge over Hawk Creek and a nearby intriguing cataract
Rockcastle Narrows East Loop	6.6	3.2	Moderate	Visit Vanhook Cascade and Vanhook Falls. From there, turn down the scenic Cane Creek Valley to reach the Rockcastle River
Cane Creek via Bald Rock Picnic Area	5.3	2.7	Moderate	This out and back trek affords solitude and wildflower viewing opportunities

Hike	Distance (miles)	Time (hours)	Difficulty	Highlights
Bee Rock Loop	5.6	2.5	Moderate	Cross historic bridge over the Rockcastle River then climb to a vista from Bee Rock, loop back along Rockcastle River
Falls of Pounder Branch and Vanhook Falls	5.2	2.5	Moderate	This hike features several waterfalls along its length, culminating in a visit to Vanhook Falls, an especially scenic spiller
Laurel River Lake Loop	3.0	1.4	Easy	Enjoy nature trails in the greater Holly Bay Recreation Area to fashion a lakeside loop
Flatwoods Trail	2.9	1.4	Easy	This hike explores the shores of regal Laurel River Lake, gaining many an aquatic vista as it makes a loop
The Scuttle Hole	2.7	1.5	Moderate	Highlights include three lake overlooks, multiple waterfalls and the Scuttle Hole
Lakeside South Loop	8.5	4.5	Moderate-difficult	Rewarding circuit hike includes lakeside woods with watery views, intimate stream valleys, cascades, and backpacking
Beaver Creek Wilderness Loop	4.1	2.5	Difficult	Hike the rugged Beaver Creek Wilderness, characterized by faint trails, little signage and challenging conditions
Bark Camp Creek Cascades	5.8	3.0	Moderate	Bark Camp Creek presents waterfalls, regal clifflines and arresting rockhouses, also visit Bark Camp Creek trail shelter
Dog Slaughter Falls Star Creek Falls and Shelter	7.6	4.0	Moderate-difficult	This gorgeous hike visits waterways big and small as well as waterfalls big and small, plus a trail shelter
Cumberland Falls Dog Slaughter Falls	7.0	3.8	Moderate-difficult	Visit two of Kentucky's most scenic waterfalls and the wild Cumberland River through a gorge of magnificent beauty
Eagle Falls Cumberland Falls	2.2	1.5	Moderate	"Must-do" hike takes you to rumbling Cumberland Falls and regal Eagle Falls, along with vistas of the Cumberland River

Hike	Distance (miles)	Time (hours)	Difficulty	Highlights
Blue Bend Loop	4.6	2.1	Moderate	This circuit hike offers a little bit of everything, a state nature preserve, old homesites, riverside terrain and waterfall
Natural Arch Scenic Area and Loop	6.5	3.5	Moderate	Easy walk to view massive Natural Arch, a bridge-like sandstone span then join the Buffalo Valley Loop with additional arch
North Fork Big Creek Falls	4.8	2.3	Easy-moderate	Hike to an incredible semi-circular rockhouse mixed with big boulders and highlighted by North Fork Big Creek Falls
Barren Fork Heritage Trail	.7	.4	Easy	Take all-accessible trail on a short loop through what once was the heart of an early Kentucky coal mining camp
Yahoo Falls Yahoo Arch	2.8	1.8	Easy	Explores Kentucky's highest cataract—Yahoo Falls—as well as an overlook of the Big South Fork and fascinating Yahoo Arch
Markers Arch Yahoo Arch	2.6	1.5	Easy	The hike visits two natural arches located near to one another in the southern end of the Daniel Boone National Forest
Lick Creek Falls Princess Falls	7.4	4.2	Moderate-difficult	View 3 distinctly different waterfalls—Lick Creek Falls, Lower Lick Creek Falls and Princess Falls—each making worthwhile destinations.
Marks Branch Falls Gobblers Knob Loop	6.1	3.6	Moderate	Valley-and-ridge circuit visits Marks Branch Falls, crisscrosses Marks Branch, then climbs to Gobblers Arch
Buffalo Arch	1.6	0.9	Easy	Join remote Parkers Mountain Trail to Buffalo Arch Trail and view stone span near Tennessee state line

Suggested Hikes

BEST HIKES FOR ARCHES
Furnace Arch --- 1
Double Arch --- 5
Grays Arch D Boon Hut --- 13
Natural Bridge Loop --- 49

BEST HIKES FOR CHILDREN
Indian Arch --- 25
Angel Windows Whistling Arch Sky Bridge --- 32
Bark Camp Creek Cascades --- 112
Yahoo Falls Yahoo Arch --- 145

BEST HIKES FOR OVERLOOKS
Double Arch --- 5
Courthouse Rock Loop --- 9
Princess Arch Chimney Top Rock --- 21
Bee Rock Loop --- 85

BEST HIKES FOR SOLITUDE
Turkey Foot Loop --- 63
Hawk Creek Suspension Bridge and Falls --- 71
Rockcastle Narrows East Loop --- 77
Beaver Creek Wilderness Loop --- 108

BEST HIKES FOR WATERFALLS
Falls of Pounder Branch & Van Hook Falls --- 89
Cumberland Falls Dog Slaughter Falls --- 122
Eagle Falls Cumberland Falls --- 127
Lick Creek Falls Princess Falls --- 154

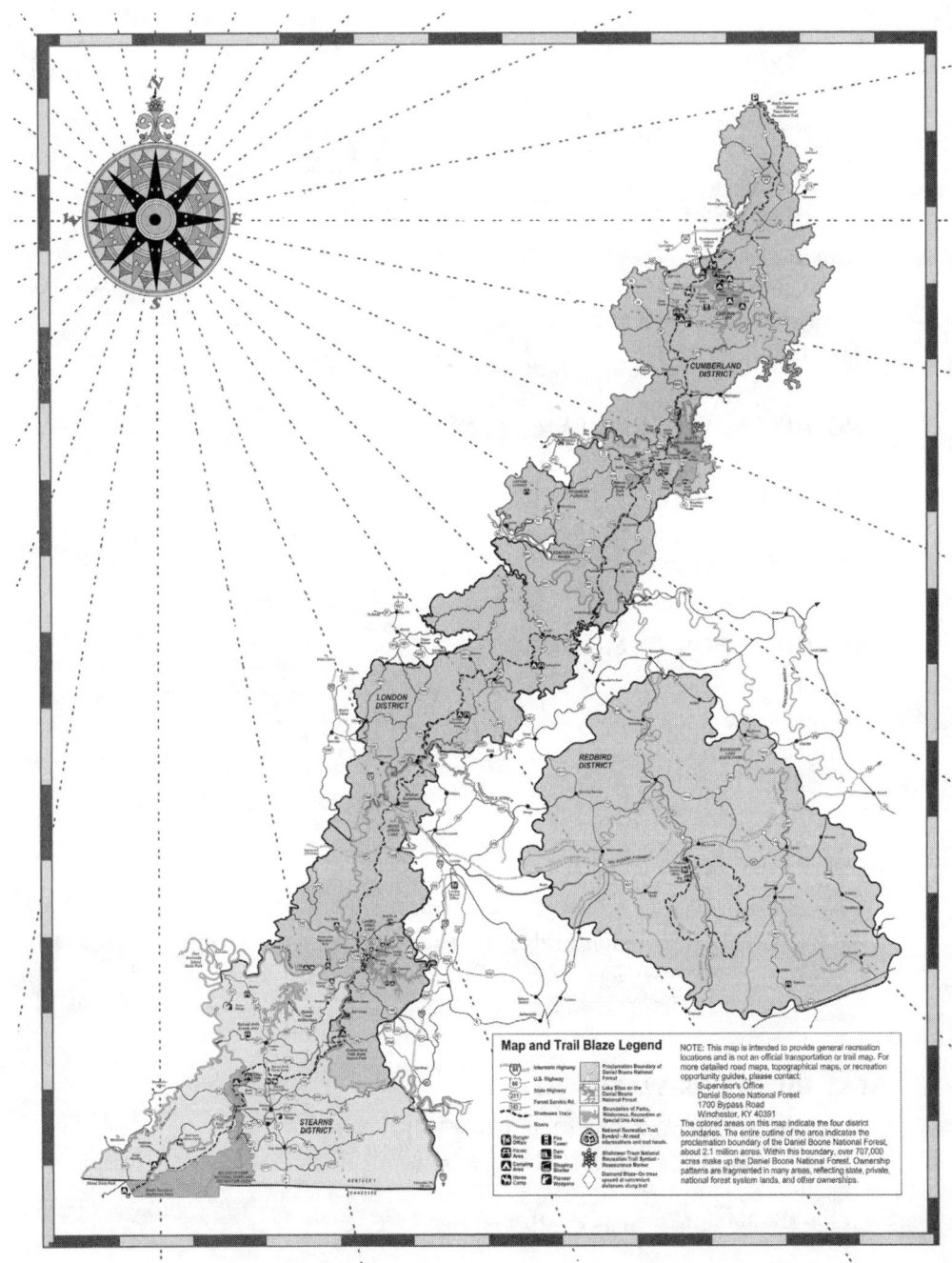

Source: Daniel Boone National Forest website. https://www.fs.usda.gov/dbnf.

DAY HIKING THE
DANIEL BOONE NATIONAL FOREST

Red River Gorge and Cave Run Lake Area

FURNACE ARCH

Hike Summary: This hike starts at worthy Clear Creek Lake Recreation Area, with its historic iron furnace, picnic area, lake and campground. The trek uses the iconic Sheltowee Trace to surmount a ridgeline then journey its wooded and rocky heights to reach fascinating Furnace Arch. Not only do you get to view the stone span but you can climb atop it for a view reaching seemingly all the way to the Ohio River. Enjoy other sporadic vistas along the way.

DISTANCE: 6.0 miles
HIKING TIME: 3.0 hours
DIFFICULTY: Moderate, does have good climb at hike beginning
HIGHLIGHTS: Furnace Arch, views, Clear Creek iron furnace
CAUTIONS: None
FEES/PERMITS: None
OTHER TRAIL USERS: Some equestrians
TRAIL CONTACTS: Cumberland Ranger District, 2375 KY 801 South, Morehead, KY 40351, (606) 784-6428, www.fs.usda.gov/dbnf

Finding the trailhead: From exit 123 on I-64 near Owingsville, take US 60 East for 6.5 miles to Salt Lick. Turn right onto KY 211.

(Ignore the left turn on KY 211 that precedes the right turn.) Follow KY 211 for 3 miles to KY 129. Take a left on KY 129, Clear Creek Road, and follow it 2.4 miles (passing Clear Creek Lake) to turn right into the Clear Creek Furnace Picnic Area. Pick up the Sheltowee Trace as it bridges Clear Creek from the rear of the picnic area. GPS Trailhead Coordinates: N38° 2.968′, W83° 35.361′

This hike offers one of my favorite vistas on the entire Sheltowee Trace, Kentucky's master path, running some 323 miles from the Big South

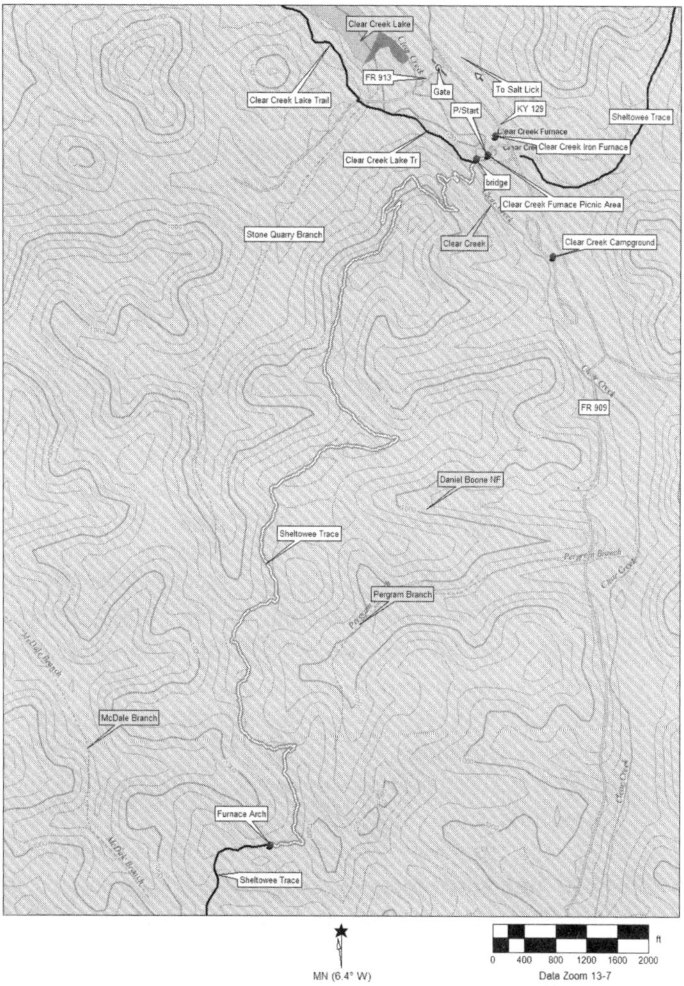

Fork National River and Recreation Area just south of the Kentucky line, all the way to Rowan County, north of Morehead, Kentucky. This particular stretch of the Sheltowee Trace trail leaves pleasant Clear Creek valley and climbs to a north-south running ridge. Your first view will be looking down on Clear Creek Lake. From there, wind southward among hardwoods to make Furnace Arch. This arch not only offers views of it, and the ability to walk beneath it, but also to walk up to the top of it and gaze into the Ohio River Valley flatlands beyond.

Leave the Clear Creek Furnace Picnic Area trailhead, crossing the metal bridge over Clear Creek, which lives up to its name. Reach a trail intersection. Here, the Clear Creek Lake Trail leaves right to circle Clear Creek Lake, which provides fishing and boating opportunities. Immediately begin ascending the nose of an unnamed ridge rising from Clear Creek. Switchbacks mitigate the very sharp grade and also minimize erosion. Do not shortcut the switchbacks. The gravelly soil is susceptible to heavy rains. Fences have been erected between some switchbacks to reduce shortcut temptation. Look back on Clear Creek Lake, visible from the switchbacks.

Rise a little under 400 feet to the ridgecrest, leveling out at .8 mile. The Sheltowee Trace soon picks up an old roadbed. Keep southbound and leave the roadbed at 1.2 miles, crossing an equestrian trail. The forest is interesting here. In places, the mature oak and tulip trees grow above a grassy floor, lending an open aspect to the woodland. Big boulders crop up along the ridgeline.

Chestnut oaks grow in the drier areas near these boulders. This particular oak is easily identified—look for thick leaves with wavy edges and a gray trunk with deeply furrowed ridges. Chestnut oaks range from Maine to Mississippi, thriving in dry, rocky upland soils such as on this ridge. Since the demise of the American chestnut, the chestnut oak's density and distribution has increased. Wildlife favors the nuts of the chestnut oak. Because of its high tannin content, the bark of this tree was once used for tanning leather.

At 1.5 miles, the Sheltowee Trace makes a hard right as it works around a knob then passes an area once mined for ore. Look for the irregular holes and disturbed ground to the right of the trail. The terrain has long since forested over, yet a keen eye will spot the non-natural location. The Sheltowee Trace winds among the oaks and mammoth rocks, up and around knobs of the ridge, keeping southbound.

At 2.7 miles, come alongside a little cliffline then make a sharp right curve, climbing over rock to rise atop the stone knob. Resume southbound. Look right and between the trees you can gaze down the Licking River valley. Wander through a boulder garden mixed with rhododendron. At 2.9 miles, the trail descends right. Keep your eyes peeled for Furnace Arch on trail right. At 3.0 miles, above the path, stands Furnace Arch. A short track leads uphill to this red bridge of rock. The colorful rock contrasts with the mossy stone on either side of it. This is a well-proportioned classic arch, about 9 feet high and 30 feet wide. Walk under it to get the bridge effect. Next, scramble atop the arch to live the bridge effect. Walk over the flat rock to a partly open area where gnarled pines hang on for dear life. To the west, Salt Lick Creek Valley is immediately below and the greater Licking River Valley leads northwest to the Ohio

River. Other ridges and valleys meld into the distance. Most visitors will be surprised such views can be had in this northern section of the Daniel Boone National Forest.

While here, make sure and check out the Clear Creek Iron Furnace, built in 1839. The furnace stands in the fine picnic area, where this hike starts. It used limonite, an ore mined in these hills that produced a very durable iron and was used to make wheels for railroad cars. In 1857, production of iron ceased but was resumed in 1873 until it was permanently shut down following a financial panic in 1875. Overnighting at Clear Creek Campground is another winning option.

MILEAGES

0.0	Clear Creek Furnace Picnic Area
0.8	Level out atop ridge
1.5	Pass former mined area
2.7	Sharp right turn atop rock
2.9	Boulder garden
3.0	Furnace Arch
6.0	Clear Creek Furnace Picnic Area

DOUBLE ARCH

Hike Summary: This hike may surprise you. Located in the Red River Gorge, the adventure follows a closed forest road atop a stone ridge, making for easy hiking, where you easily appreciate the trailside scenery. Next drop below the ridgeline, walking rich woods in the shadow of rock palisades. Circle around a tan stone massif then climb to Double Arch. This span is actually two arches on top of one another, with the lower arch a narrow, slit-like opening, and the upper arch thick span. After viewing the span from below climb the Double Arch and walk a sandstone knob for stellar views of the Red River Gorge.

DISTANCE: 4.8-mile there-and-back
HIKING TIME: 2.4 hours
DIFFICULTY: Moderate
HIGHLIGHTS: Double Arch, views from atop Double Arch
FEES/PERMITS: Permit required if camping in the Red River Gorge between 10 p.m. and 6 a.m.
OTHER TRAIL USERS: None
TRAIL CONTACTS: Cumberland Ranger District, 2375 KY 801 South, Morehead, KY 40351, (606) 784-6428, www.fs.usda.gov/dbnf

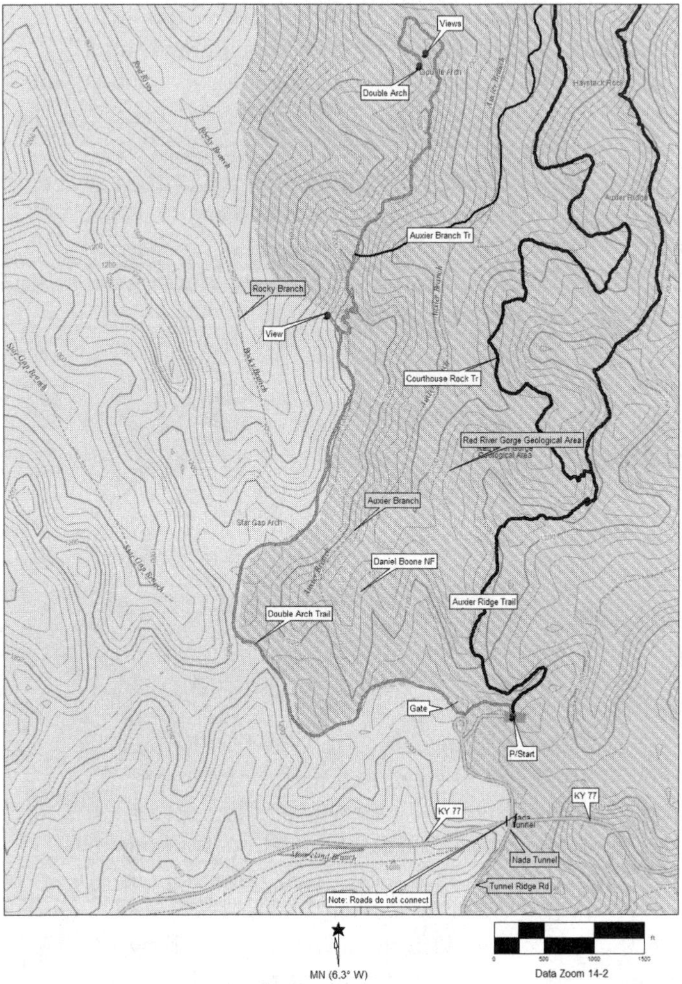

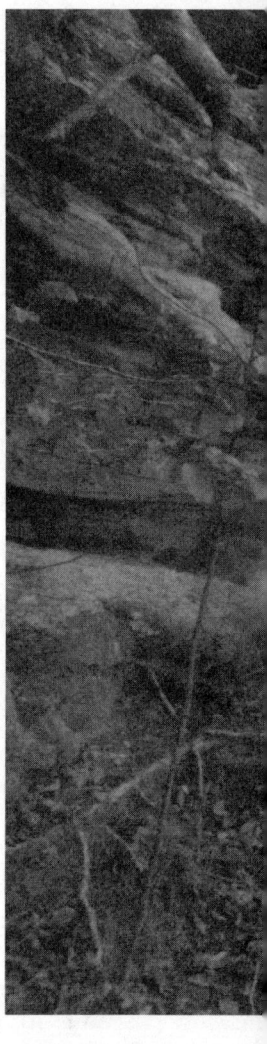

Finding the trailhead: From exit 33 on the Mountain Parkway near Slade, take KY 15 south for 3.3 miles to turn left on Tunnel Ridge Road. Follow Tunnel Ridge Road for 3.7 miles to dead end at the Auxier trailhead. Note: You cannot access the trailhead from KY 77 near Nada Tunnel. GPS Trailhead Coordinates: N37° 49.203', W83° 40.855'

Many of the trails within the Daniel Boone National Forest are rugged narrow paths scrambling along clifflines, twisting through boulder

clogged streams and up sandstone ledges and along still more variations of rugged terrain. The pathways sometimes replicate obstacle courses as they maneuver through the geological phenomena within the Cumberland Plateau that characterizes much of Eastern Kentucky. Therefore, it can be a pleasant surprise when you take a hike and much of the trail is a foot friendly walk in the woods, but still leading to yet another intriguing geological feature that makes the Daniel Boone National Forest so special.

It is Double Arch in this case. As its name implies the stone span highlights a sizeable stone span topped with a parallel arch below it, more of a narrow, window-type arch. I recommend visiting Double Arch in the morning or evening when sunlight hits the arch at a low angle, sending rays of light through the two arch openings.

Start your hike to Double Arch at the Auxier trailhead, with a large parking area and restroom. The signed Double Arch Trail begins next to the Auxier Ridge Trail. Follow the singletrack path west to join gated Tunnel Ridge Road, FR 201, at .1 mile. The Double Arch Trail runs in conjunction with the gated forest road for a ways, under a forest of chestnut oaks, sourwood, and red maple, with scattered cedars and pines. The head of the Auxier Branch valley drops steeply to your right. Stay atop the ridgeline dividing Auxier Branch to your right and Rocky Branch to your left, both tributaries of the Red River.

User-created spur trails head to backcountry campsites but since you are on a closed forest road there is no mistaking them for the correct route. At 1.3 miles, the forest becomes more sparse overhead. At 1.4 miles, come to a trail intersection. Here, the closed forest road ends at a turnaround and view ahead. Split right, now joining a signed singletrack footpath diving into the craggy Auxier Branch valley. Switchbacks lead you down to the base of the ridge, where stone palisades rise high above. The vegetation reflects the moister conditions down here—magnolia, hemlock and tulip trees, along with healthy doses of ferns and moss.

Cruise along the base of a monolithic cliffline, a stone rampart forming the foundation of this land. At 1.7 miles, intersect the Auxier Branch Trail. It leaves right, across Auxier Branch then meets the Courthouse Rock Trail. Our hike stays left with the Double Arch Trail, and continues to circle around the stone upthrust from which Double Arch is formed. At 1.8 miles, the path bridges a trickling creeklet emanating from the base of the stone pillar. By 2.2 miles, you are circling around the rock rampart, then curve back south.

Stone steps lead to Double Arch, which you reach at 2.4 miles. Enjoy the up close look at the span standing about 10 feet high and 20 or more feet wide. The upper arch stands above a substantial rockhouse open on both sides, with a dusty floor. Below it, the lower arch has but a foot or two between the upper and lower tiers, and adds a delicate aspect to the sturdy stone span. Examine it from multiple angles. Arch fans also like to view Double Arch atop nearby Auxier Ridge, from which the two stone spans and the large void below the arches is clearly visible.

Next climb atop Double Arch, using steps carved in the sandstone on the right hand side as you approach. From there, cross the arch and keep north as an open stone knob avails panoramas throughout the Red River Gorge. Courthouse Rock stands above the trees across Auxier Branch, as do other rock upthrusts while the Red River meanders through the lowermost tree-covered vale below. This is a spot to linger, and to appreciate the beauty found within the Daniel Boone National Forest.

MILEAGES

0.0   Auxier trailhead
1.4   Leave right from Forest Road, view nearby
1.7   Auxier Branch Trail leaves right
2.4   Double Arch
4.8   Auxier trailhead

COURTHOUSE ROCK LOOP

Hike Summary: This is a view-rich loop, complemented with close up beauty as well. Take the Auxier Ridge Trail, much of which traces a narrow sandstone ridgetop with sporadic tree cover, opening up view after view after view of the surrounding Red River Gorge. Special vistas include that of Haystack Rock, Double Arch

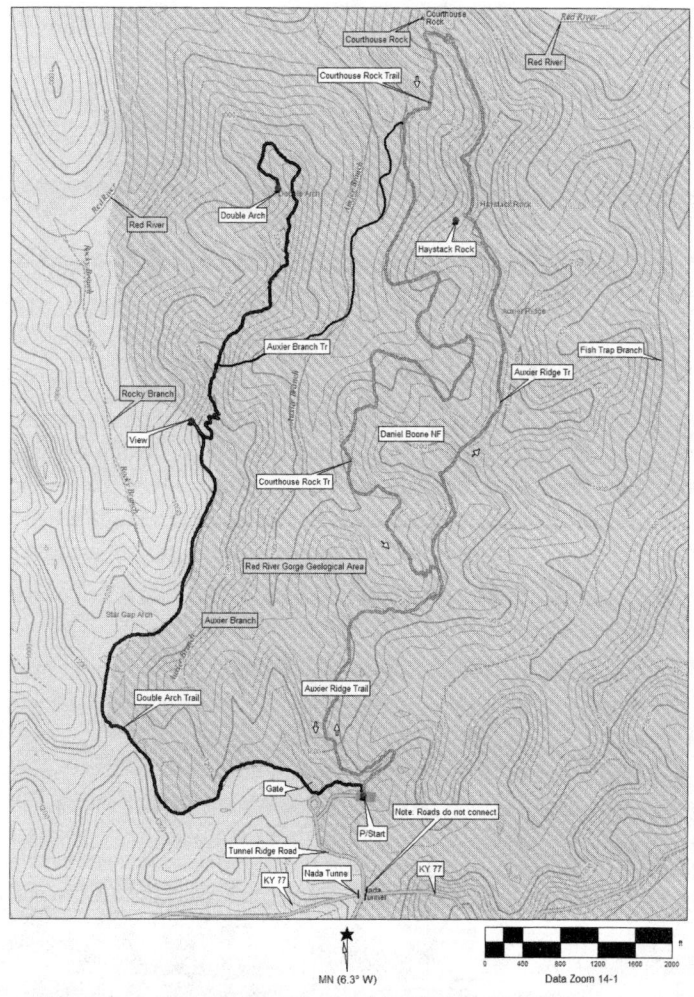

and Courthouse Rock. Make your way to the base of Courthouse Rock then turn south on the Courthouse Rock Trail, meandering below the bluffs upon which you just walked, adding a change of scenery to finally backtrack to the trailhead.

DISTANCE: 5.1-mile balloon loop
HIKING TIME: 2.6 hours
DIFFICULTY: Moderate
HIGHLIGHTS: Multiple views of Double Arch, Haystack Rock, and Courthouse Rock

FEES/PERMITS: Permit required if camping in the Red River Gorge between 10 p.m. and 6 a.m.
OTHER TRAIL USERS: None
TRAIL CONTACTS: Cumberland Ranger District, 2375 KY 801 South, Morehead, KY 40351, (606) 784-6428, www.fs.usda.gov/dbnf

Finding the trailhead: From exit 33 on the Mountain Parkway near Slade, take KY 15 south for 3.3 miles to turn left on Tunnel Ridge Road. Follow Tunnel Ridge Road for 3.7 miles to dead end at the Auxier trailhead. GPS Trailhead Coordinates: N37° 49.203', W83° 40.855'

If you are looking for a hike in the Red River Gorge that offers many views then this is it. The hike first takes the Auxier Ridge Trail. Auxier Ridge is replete with rock outcrops from which you can see other sandstone protrusions rising above the woods of the Red River Gorge, as well as the hollows and ridges of the Red River drainage. Among the emergent sandstone ledges, knobs and ridges you will be able to easily identify three major geological points of interest—Haystack Rock, Double Arch and Courthouse Rock, all from differing distances and angles.

Start the popular trek from the Auxier trailhead, a potentially busy starting point (Consider doing this hike during off times to avoid crowds). Leave north from the parking area on the Auxier Ridge Trail. Head northeast circling around a stony pillar. Briefly turn southwest at .1 mile, passing by a rockhouse before turning back north on a narrow ridgeline, populated with scattered sourwood, shortleaf pine and black gum, with vegetation absent from patches of sandstone. At .5 miles, sandstone steps have been carved into the ridge to aid your passage. Ahead, look for a notable mushroom shaped rock directly in the middle of the path.

Views are opening along the trail from the sandstone slabs. The hollows created by Fish Trap Branch below to your right and Auxier Branch to your left yield looks at stone and wood ridges in the distance. The views come fast and furious as the trail angles northeast, then back north again, sporting scant tree cover. Woe to the hiker tackling this trail on a sunny August afternoon.

At .9 mile, come to the intersection with the Courthouse Rock Trail. This will be your return route. For now, keep straight on the Auxier Ridge Trail, soaking in more forest, rock and sky, as the panoramas continue. Look on the lower trunks of trees on Auxier Ridge for telltale black marks, revealing past burnings. Undulate on the crest, passing through some sections of wider, more forested ridgeline.

At 1.7 miles, open onto a memorable view that many hikers associate with being in the Red River Gorge. A huge sandstone flat stretches to the rim of the ridge that is your 180-degree viewing platform. The unusual cylindrical form of Haystack Rock with its trademark mini-knob protrudes below you. The unmistakable Double Arch stands across the chasm of Auxier Branch. The Red River runs through the lowlands below while the highlands of Ratton Ridge form a backdrop of stone and forest.

You are heading north and can see down to the Red River below. By 2.1 miles, come to the end of Auxier Ridge. A partly vegetated outcrop allows a look to the north. It is 400 feet down to the Red River while the now-close Courthouse Rock rises for the sky above. Rock climbers come out here to scale its heights. On the overlook itself, look for an eroded rock with its base narrow than its top, eventually to succumb to time and the elements, but standing for now.

From here, descend an incredible set of steps including a curved stairwell that leads from the cap rock of Auxier Ridge down to the base of its clifflines. Reach a gap between the top of Auxier Ridge and Courthouse Ridge. A user created trail heads north toward the base of Courthouse Rock while the signed Courthouse Rock Trail descends and briefly heads north before turning back south to meander below the west-facing sandstone pillars of Auxier Ridge.

Meet the Auxier Branch Trail at 2.4 miles. It leaves right to cross Auxier Branch and connect to the Double Arch Trail. A side trip to Double Arch could make a rewarding extension to this hike, adding about 3 miles total distance from here if you went to Double Arch and back to this trail intersection.

This hike continues on the Courthouse Rock Trail, crossing intermittent drainages flowing from Auxier Ridge. Pick up an old logging road, circling into other drainages, some thick with rhododendron. Split away from the old logging road on an irregular singletrack path. Make the final push back to the top of Auxier Ridge on a rough trail mitigated by switchbacks, finally meeting the Auxier Ridge Trail at 4.2 miles. From here it is a .9 mile backtrack to the trailhead, completing this view-laden hike.

MILEAGES

0.0   Auxier trailhead
0.9   Pass intersection with Courthouse Rock Trail
1.7   Superlative view above Haystack Rock
2.1   View of Courthouse Rock, steps, intersection with Courthouse Rock Trail

2.4   Auxier Branch Trail leaves right
4.2   Right on Auxier Ridge Trail
5.1   Auxier trailhead

GRAYS ARCH D BOON HUT

Hike Summary: This hike visits two major highlights—geologically significant Grays Arch and historically significant D Boon Hut. Grays Arch is one of the most picturesque arches in the Red River Gorge and is a popular day hiking destination. The hike also takes you into and out of stream valleys and past overlooks extending into adjacent parts of the Red River gorge.

DISTANCE: 4.7-mile loop
HIKING TIME: 2.3 hours
DIFFICULTY: Moderate
HIGHLIGHTS: D Boon Hut, Grays Arch
FEES/PERMITS: Permit required if camping in the Red River Gorge between 10 p.m. and 6 a.m.
OTHER TRAIL USERS: None
TRAIL CONTACTS: Cumberland Ranger District, 2375 KY 801 South, Morehead, KY 40351, (606) 784-6428, www.fs.usda.gov/dbnf

Finding the trailhead: From exit 33 on the Mountain Parkway near Slade, take KY 15 south for 3.3 miles to turn left on Tunnel Ridge Road. Follow Tunnel Ridge Road for .9 mile to Grays Arch picnic area and trailhead. GPS Trailhead Coordinates: N37° 48.446′, W83° 39.477′

This loop has many ups and downs as it leads you past Grays Arch and D Boon Hut among other highlights, so expect a little vertical challenge along the way. Your first descent begins immediately en route to D Boon Hut. Here, you find a rock shelter where potassium nitrate, once commonly known as "niter" and "saltpeter," was mined for the making of gunpowder and perhaps ol' Daniel Boone himself used the shelter as a winter hunt camp. The hike then climbs to a ridge where Grays Arch is found. This massive, high stone bridge has a substantial curving span and its setting near a huge stone shelter constructs a wild scene. The hike then drops to King Branch only to immediately climb away. The final part of the trek loops back on Rush Ridge, where views can be had into the Red River Gorge.

Start the hike by leaving the Grays Arch Picnic Area on the D Boon Hut Trail, which begins at the southwest end of the Grays Arch Picnic Area, next to Tunnel Ridge Road. Join a singletrack path descending, using a plethora of steps, nearing a huge curve rock shelter. At .3 mile, bridge a springlet flowing from a cliffline above. Rhododendron and magnolia

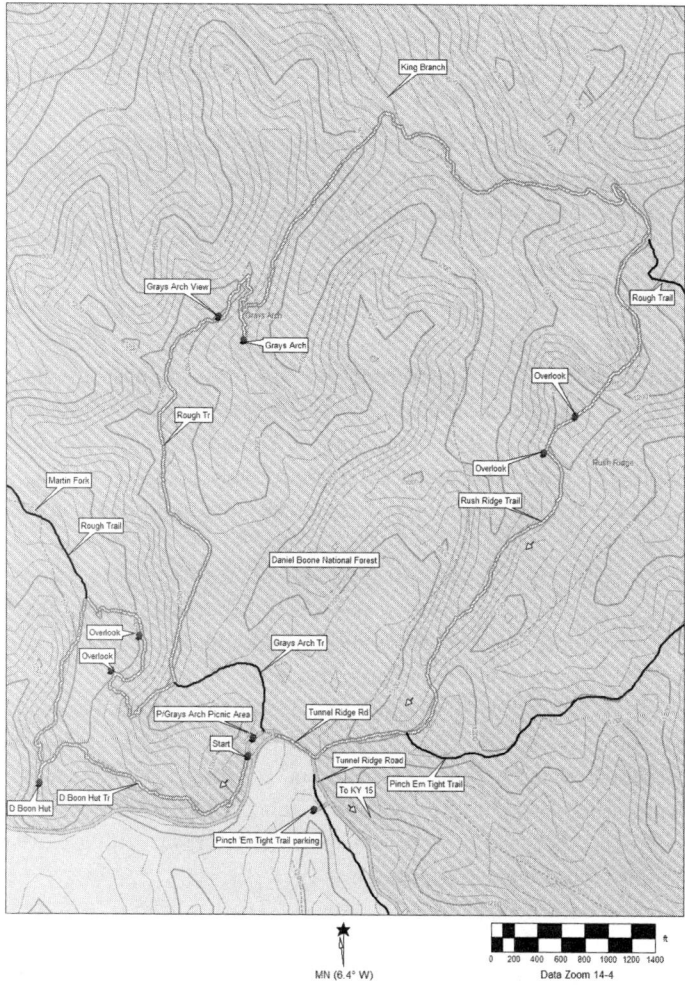

grow in abundance. At .4 mile, take the left spur leading to D Boon Hut. Cruise along a massive sandstone cliffline before coming to the huge stone shelter known as D Boon Hut at .5 mile.

This we know for sure, in the early 1800s and again during the Civil War, a niter mining operation took place here. Potassium nitrate crystals were extracted from the sandstone, then taken to powder mills in Lexington among other places to make gunpowder. The back of the shelter is fenced off yet you can still see the remains of the wooden troughs and crude fireplaces used in this operation.

Now whether Daniel Boone himself camped here or not is much less certain. In 1959, someone found the name "D Boon" inscribed onto a board of a hut under the rock shelter. From this sprung the legend that Kentucky's first son used this particular rock shelter as a winter hunt camp. Subsequent examinations of the purported carving and construction of a hut in the shelter have called a Boone stay here into question. Supposed carvings by Daniel Boone can be found all over the Bluegrass State and almost all are likely forgeries. Nevertheless, the name D Boon Hut has been attached to this shelter and mine site.

Backtrack to the main path and intersect the Rough Trail at .9 mile, after bridging Martin Fork. Turn right here, climbing to find an outcrop at 1.1 miles, with a view down Martin Fork. Quickly pass a second view, this time of Auxier Ridge and climb further, working over sandstone slabs to meet the Grays Arch Trail at 1.3 miles. You are but a quarter-mile from the parking area but stay with the Rough Trail, aiming for Grays Arch. Enjoy the most level segment of the hike on a wide trail under pines and oaks.

At 2.0 miles, find a view of Grays Arch. Here, you can peer across a hollow at the massive sandstone span rising in silhouette against the sky. This spectacle, best in winter, will quicken your pulse and make you eager to see the 79-foot wide span. Cruise along a cliffline then descend into a vale to reach a trail intersection. Here, the Rough Trail continues left but you stay straight, heading for Grays Arch. Enter an alcove with an enormous rock shelter, fronted by a dripping low volume cascade. Climb past the cascade outflow then reach the base of Grays Arch at 2.3 miles. Walk under and around the span, with other geological wonders about. The arch is very high above you.

Backtrack then continue the Rough Trail. Descend to cross King Branch at 2.8 miles, then cross twice more in quick succession. Here comes another climb. Work your way up a thickly vegetated hollow then turn uphill on seemingly endless stairs. Level out on Rush Ridge and reach a trail intersection at 3.5 miles. Here, keep straight, joining the Rush Ridge Trail, as the Rough Trail splits left. Head south amid oak, maple, sourwood and shortleaf pine. Pass a pair of overlooks at 3.8 and 3.9 miles, where you can stand on sandstone edges and soak in the stone and forest of the Red River Gorge.

At 4.5 miles, meet the Pinch Em Tight Trail and stay right. Emerge onto Tunnel Ridge Road at 4.6 miles. From here, turn right and follow gravel Tunnel Ridge Road for .1 mile, returning to the Grays Arch Picnic Area trailhead.

MILEAGES

0.0	Grays Arch Picnic Area trailhead
0.4	Spur to D Boon Hut
0.5	D Boon Hut
0.9	Right on Rough Trail
1.3	Pass intersection with Grays Arch Trail
2.0	View of Grays Arch
2.3	Grays Arch
3.5	Join Rush Ridge Trail
4.5	Pinch Em Tight Trail
4.6	Tunnel Ridge Road
4.7	Grays Arch Picnic Area trailhead

CHIMNEY TOP CREEK HIKE

Hike Summary: This hike displays some of the best everywhere-you-look beauty contained within the Red River Gorge. Start deep within the gorge on the Sheltowee Trace. Hike along the Red River, then cross it on a swinging bridge. From there, enjoy more riverside walking before turning up clear Chimney Top Creek, a gorgeous stream and valley. Next, head up the Right Fork Chimney Creek valley. While over there, soak in a big view from a big sandstone slab. Finally loop back to the Sheltowee Trace, recrossing the Red River.

DISTANCE: 9.0 miles balloon loop
HIKING TIME: 5 hours
DIFFICULTY: Difficult due to distance, many ups and downs
HIGHLIGHTS: Sheltowee Trace suspension bridge, Red River, Chimney Top Creek, views
CAUTIONS: Bridgeless creek crossings
FEES/PERMITS: Permit required if camping in the Red River Gorge between 10 p.m. and 6 a.m.
OTHER TRAIL USERS: None
TRAIL CONTACTS: Cumberland Ranger District, 2375 KY 801 South, Morehead, KY 40351, (606) 784-6428, www.fs.usda.gov/dbnf

Finding the trailhead: From exit 33 on the Mountain Parkway near Slade, head north on KY 11 for 1.5 miles to turn right onto KY 77 north. Follow it for 5.1 miles to KY 715, passing through Nada

Tunnel and bridging the Red River along the way. Turn right on KY 715 south and follow it for 1.5 miles to make the right turn down to the Sheltowee Trace suspension bridge trailhead at .2 mile. GPS Trailhead Coordinates: N37° 49.381', W83° 37.689'

This is one of my favorite hikes in the Red River Gorge. The beauty starts from the first step and continues the whole way, from looking down on the Red River, one of Kentucky's finest aquatic treasures, to the magnificent wildflowers and forests of the Chimney Top Creek valley, to the views from cliffs above the valleys.

Leave the suspension bridge parking area joining the Sheltowee Trace Connector, heading upstream along the Red River. Squeeze between a low bluff to your left and the waterway to your right, riddled with massive boulders, gravel bars and overhanging trees. At .4 mile, meet the Sheltowee Trace. Here, turn right, immediately crossing the massive hiker suspension bridge. Enjoy river views from atop the span. Turn back downstream in flats of ash, sycamore and pawpaw, circling below Chimney Top Rock.

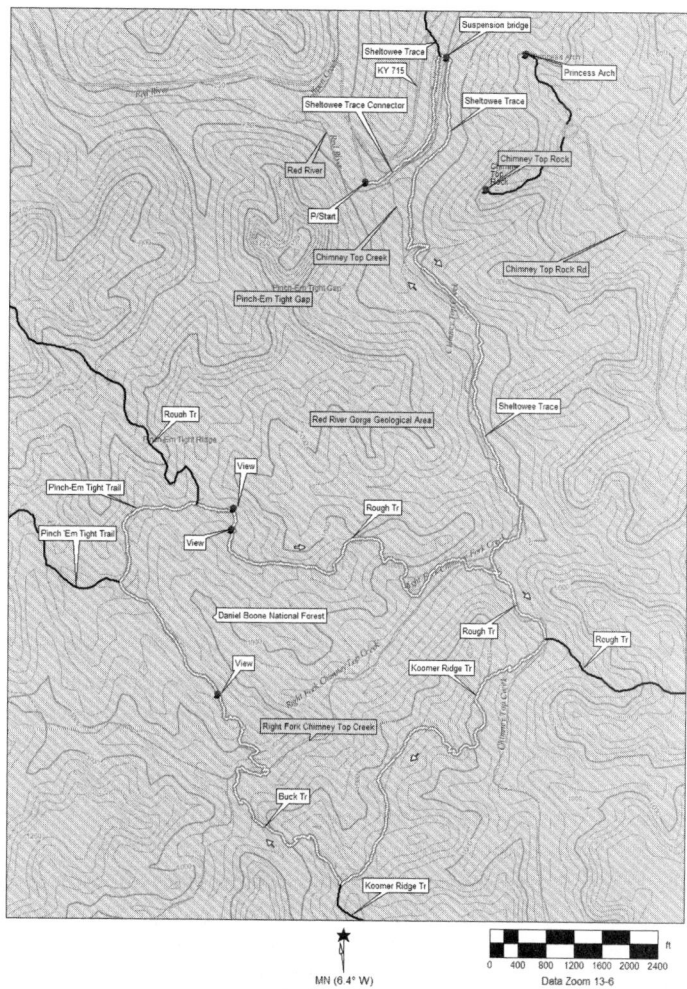

At .8-mile turn into the Chimney Top Creek hollow. At 1.1 miles, step over a tributary of Chimney Top Creek. From here, surprisingly climb by switchbacks, once again rising well above Chimney Top Creek, only to return to streamside flats at 1.4 miles. Enjoy the beauty of this crystalline stream and the flora around it. At 1.9 miles, make a pair of quick crossings of Chimney Top Creek, likely to be wet fords in spring. At 2.2 miles, in an evergreen flat above the confluence of Chimney Top Creek and Right Fork Chimney Top Creek, reach a trail junction and the loop portion of the hike. From here, head left on the Rough Trail, continuing up Chimney Top Creek.

Big boulders litter the stream. Tulip trees and white pines stand overhead. Cross the creek again at 2.3 miles then reach another trail intersection. Here, the Rough Trail crosses back over the creek but we stay right, joining the Koomer Ridge Trail at 2.4 miles, still going up Chimney Top Creek. Pass more massive streamside boulders. At 2.6 miles, steeply climb then turn away from the creek entirely, ascending a piney ridge to level off at 3.0 miles. Roll south among blueberries, greenbrier and rhododendron thickets.

At 3.6 miles, turn right onto the Buck Trail. Cruise through pines before descending into the Right Fork Chimney Creek hollow, where moisture-loving vegetation predominates. Come to the stream at 4.1 miles, making three quick crossings in the depths of the mossy, ferny creek then quickly and steeply climb away from the sparkling stream, back into xeric woodland of pine, oak and sourwood. At 4.7 miles, pass a partial view to east, down the Chimney Top Creek valley. The Buck Trail negotiates a slender forested ridge, sometimes crossing sandstone slabs.

At 5.1 miles, turn right onto the Pinch 'Em Tight Trail, with which the Sheltowee Trace runs in conjunction. Head north on a pine and stone ridge that is the highest on the hike. At 5.4 miles, come to yet another intersection. Here, you turn right on the Rough Trail, with which the Sheltowee Trace also runs. This ridge also is heavy with sandstone among the often-low tree cover. At 5.6 miles, open onto another view from a sandstone outcrop. Here, you can scope easterly down the Chimney Creek hollow to the Red River and beyond. Briefly hike through woods then open onto a very large sandstone slab—bare naked rock. Ironically, though the slab is impressive, the views are lesser. A host of visitors has inscribed their names in the slab, a practice frowned upon these days by the Forest Service.

At 6.1 miles, you are in full descent toward Right Fork Chimney Top Creek and by 6.3 miles, you are alongside the waterway in a rich flowery gulch. At 6.6 miles, come to the crossing of Right Fork Chimney Top Creek, where stepping stones are lined up to make dry footing a higher possibility. Meander flats under walnut, sycamore and tulip trees. The confluence of Right Fork and Chimney Top Creeks lies to your left. Make the crossing of Chimney Top Creek just before completing the loop portion of the hike at 6.8 miles. From here, turn left onto the Sheltowee Trace and backtrack 2.2 miles to the trailhead, completing the hike.

Mileages

0.0	Sheltowee Trace suspension bridge trailhead
0.4	Right on Sheltowee Trace
2.2	Left on Rough Trail

2.4	Right on Koomer Ridge Trail
3.6	Right on Buck Trail
4.7	Easterly view
5.1	Right on Pinch 'Em Tight Trail
5.4	Right on Rough Trail
5.6	View into Red River Gorge
6.8	Complete loop, backtrack
9.0	Sheltowee Trace suspension bridge trailhead

PRINCESS ARCH CHIMNEY TOP ROCK

Hike Summary: This Red River Gorge experience combines two short and scenic nature trails starting from the same picnic area. First, walk out along a ridgetop to what I believe is the best vista point in the entire Red River Gorge, Chimney Top Rock. Look out on the river itself and the stone pocked highlands rising from the waterway itself. After returning from that adventure, leave the picnic area a second time, this time aiming for Princess Arch. Cruise a second ridgeline to reach long, slender Princess Arch. First, walk under the span and take a loop trail to another view of the Red River Gorge before returning back, walking atop Princess Arch.

DISTANCE: Two .6-mile nature trails
HIKING TIME: .8 hour
DIFFICULTY: Easy
HIGHLIGHTS: Views from Chimney Top Rock, Princess Arch
FEES/PERMITS: Permit required if camping in the Red River Gorge between 10 p.m. and 6 a.m.
OTHER TRAIL USERS: None
TRAIL CONTACTS: Cumberland Ranger District, 2375 KY 801 South, Morehead, KY 40351, (606) 784-6428, www.fs.usda.gov/dbnf

Finding the trailhead: From exit 40 on the Mountain Parkway near Pine Ridge, take KY 15 north for 1.3 miles to turn right on KY 715 north. Follow KY 715 north for 2.2 miles to split left on Forest Road 10. Follow gravel Forest Road 10 for 3.6 miles to dead end at the Chimney Rock Picnic Area. GPS Trailhead Coordinates: N37° 49.4847', W83° 37.0848'

Chimney Top Rock and Princess Arch are two Daniel Boone National Forest hiking destinations that most anyone can reach. And since the two destinations begin at the same trailhead, it is just as easy to see both

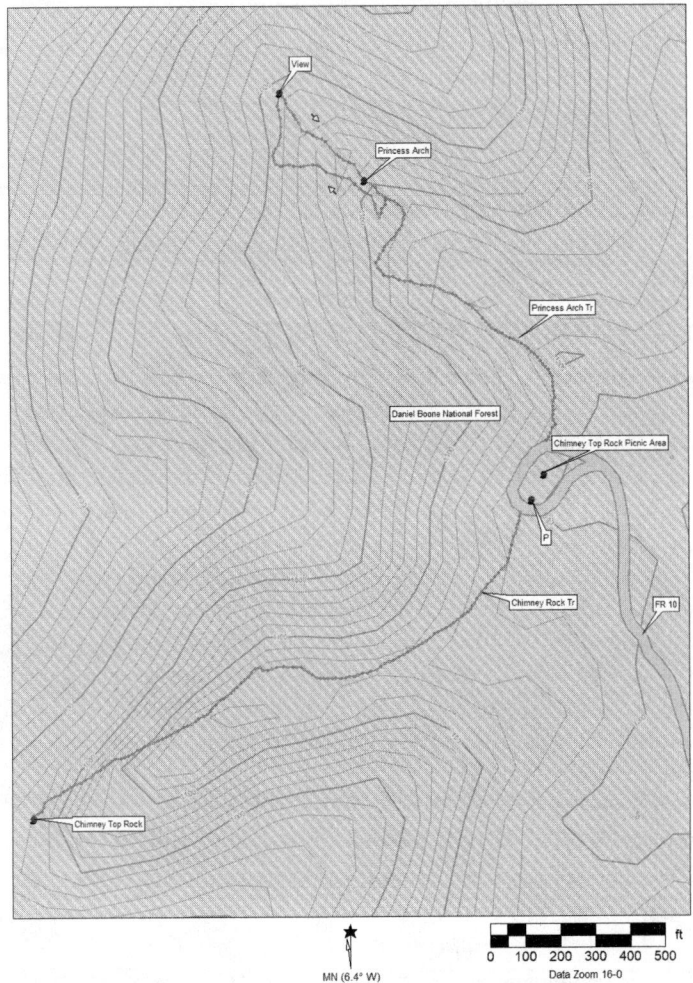

as it is one. Furthermore, the trail to Chimney Top Rock is paved to its first overlook, allowing wheelchair hikers to soak in the Red River Gorge from its heights. Onward, the official overlook affords a spectacular view of the Red River, Half Moon Rock and other standout outcrops amid the thick forests draping the gorge.

Ironically, both these seemingly easy and simple destinations have been the scene of numerous deaths. In fact, a memorial stands at the beginning of the trail to Princess Arch, a reminder of a man who fell to his death from the top of Princess Arch. Red River Gorge visitors die yearly

from falls off the seemingly innumerable cliffs within the forest, many at Chimney Top Rock, despite warning signs along the way about the danger of cliffs. The overlook is bordered by a wooden fence but visitors simply go around the fence for a better view or a better picture. Or they show off. Or they walk around at night. They follow user-created trails, not knowing exactly where they lead. Yet other deaths involve experienced and competent hikers and climbers raising their challenge to the next level—only to find that next level is actually down. But most of the accidents involve drinking and/or drug use. And a seemingly innocuous overlook like Chimney Top Rock becomes a place of perishment.

A recent death here include one man rock hopping on the edge of Chimney Top Rock, trying to span a chasm between two stone spires. Another death occurred after a drinking bout then the lush stepped beyond the bounds of the fenced view. Over 20 people have died at Chimney Top Rock since 1960. In other parts of the Red River Gorge visitors camp on the edge of an overlook and the next morning they are gone. Recently a group of four hikers walking at night fell off a cliff one after another like lemmings. They all survived but much worse for wear, terrible broken bones all around.

These accidents can be avoided with common sense and restraint, over both of which the personnel of the Daniel Boone National Forest has no control. Is it really better to plaster the wilderness with an excess of warning signs or to close off destinations such as Chimney Top Rock altogether? As the saying goes, "You can't legislate out stupidity."

Therefore, exercise caution while on these two nature walks and you will safely enjoy their offerings. First, head out on the Chimney Top Rock Trail. An asphalt path leads along a pine-oak ridge and you pass a partial overlook. The path descends a bit then a land bridge brings you to the outcrop from which so much beauty can be seen. To your left stands easily identifiable Half Moon Rock. Other outcrops rise across the Chimney Top Creek below. Look down and you can see the Red River itself, making a bend and stretching toward the horizon, flanked by stone and forest. The inspiring sight makes the numerous deaths here seem unimaginable. It is my favorite overlook in all the Red River Gorge.

Return .3 mile back to the trailhead, perhaps interspersing your adventure with a little picnic using one of the tables scattered here. Otherwise, head to the other side of the picnic area and pick up the Princess Arch Trail. Here you will see the stone memorial to the man who fell to his death from Princess Arch in 1990. Join another piney ridge, descending to reach the a narrow part of the ridge and dip left to reach Princess Arch. The slender span stretches 32 feet wide and 8 feet high. The far side of the arch overlooks a drop off.

Continue the hike and head farther out the ridge to reach a north facing overlook of the Red River Gorge. From here, the trail turns back and takes you atop Princess Arch! This way you can enjoy the geological feature from all angles. Many a photo is snapped of hikers standing atop the stone bridge. From here it is a simple backtrack to the trailhead.

Mileages
0.0   Chimney Top Rock Picnic Area trailhead
0.3   Chimney Top Rock Overlook
0.6   Chimney Top Rock Picnic Area trailhead
0.2   Princess Arch
0.3   Overlook
0.6   Chimney Top Rock Picnic Area trailhead

INDIAN ARCH

Hike Summary: Take a walk to a slender sloping arch and grab a big view from its heights. The trek uses the Bison Way Trail, named for buffalo that were once housed in a nearby meadow. Name aside, the path takes you up Sergeant Branch to meet the Sheltowee Trace. Here, the Trace meanders along streams above which tower sandstone monoliths. Curve along a steep cliffline before making a final ascent up wooden stairs to reach Indian Arch, a classic span. Stellar views wait after you climb to the top of the stone bridge.

DISTANCE: 3.0 miles
HIKING TIME: 1.6 hours
DIFFICULTY: Easy
HIGHLIGHTS: Spring wildflowers, Indian Arch, views
CAUTIONS: None
FEES/PERMITS: Permit required if camping in the Red River Gorge between 10 p.m. and 6 a.m.
OTHER TRAIL USERS: None
TRAIL CONTACTS: Cumberland Ranger District, 2375 KY 801 South, Morehead, KY 40351, (606) 784-6428, www.fs.usda.gov/dbnf

Finding the trailhead: From exit 33 on the Mountain Parkway near Slade, head north on KY 11 for 1.5 miles to turn right onto KY 77 north. Follow it for 5.1 miles to KY 715, passing through Nada Tunnel and bridging the Red River along the way. Turn right on KY 715 south and follow it for 3.2 miles to make the left turn into the Bison Way trailhead just before the road bridge over Gladie Creek. GPS Trailhead Coordinates: N37° 50.215′, W83° 36.575′

This hike begins near the Gladie Visitor Center and Historic site. There you can explore the visitor center with interpretive displays about the Daniel Boone National Forest as well as books and souvenirs. Forest personnel are on site. The visitor center is open daily from 9 a.m. to 5:30 p.m. You can also visit the Gladie cabin, a historic log structure built around 1900. Once a thriving farm with plentiful outbuildings and a swinging bridge spanning Gladie Creek, the cabin never had electricity. Interestingly however, it was lit up and heated by piped natural gas from a nearby gas well. The Daniel Boone National Forest acquired the property in 1987, restoring the cabin and refurbishing and refurnishing

the inside, replicating life in the early 1900s. Buffalo once lived in an adjacent field but were later moved to Land Between The Lakes National Recreation Area, shared by Kentucky and Tennessee well west of the Daniel Boone National Forest.

To do it all without moving your vehicle, consider parking at the visitor center, exploring it and the Gladie Cabin, walk over to the Bison Way trailhead then make the hike to Indian Arch. It is less than a quarter mile from the visitor center to the Bison Way trailhead. Once at the Bison Way trailhead, join the Bison Way Trail, a singletrack path ascending on many square stone steps. Gladie Creek flows down to your

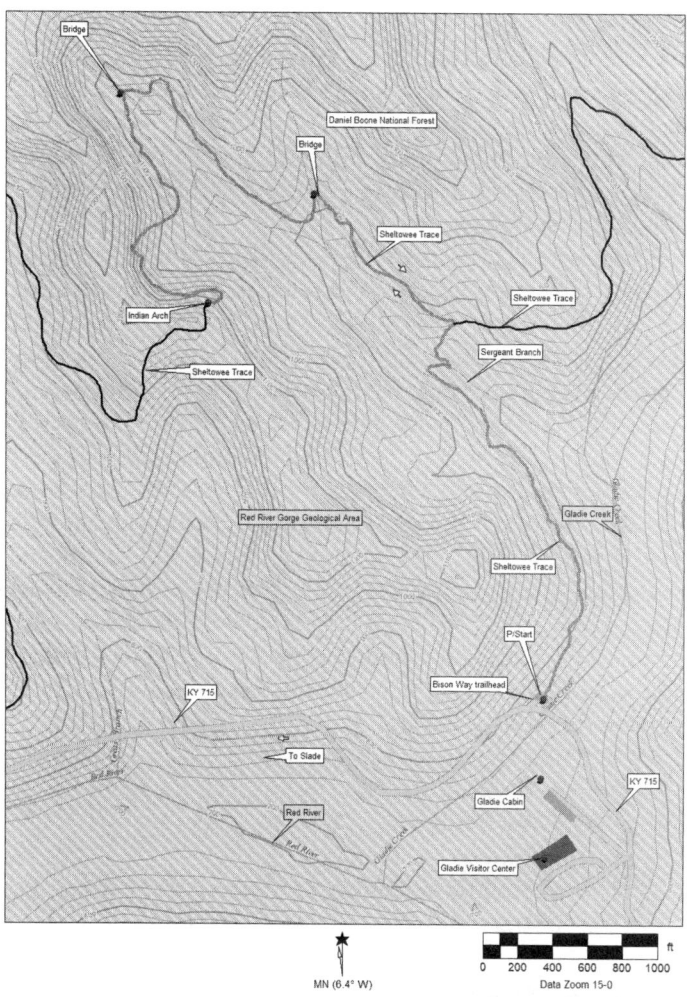

right. The hillside above you is loaded with wildflowers in spring, most notably white trillium. Ahead, step over a couple of spring seeps flowing over the trail. At .4 mile in evergreens, descend by switchbacks to rock hop Sergeant Branch, a perennial tributary of Gladie Creek, itself a tributary of Red River.

Climb away from Sergeant Branch and meet the Sheltowee Trace at .5 mile. Head left here on the Trace, southbound but actually heading northwest from the intersection. A little bit ahead, an unmaintained path heads right and uphill for the Indian Staircase, a set of stairs carved into a sloped sandstone ledge, purportedly created by pre-Columbian Kentuckians. That adventure is considered off-trail hiking.

Our hike stays with the Sheltowee Trace, crossing small branches. At .8 mile, the trail bridges an intermittent stream. Huge sandstone ledges rise above you. Continue curving around the uppermost reaches of Sergeant Branch. At 1.1 miles, bridge a streambed then another streambed in a rhododendron thicket.

The Sheltowee Trace turns south and works along a cliffline, slowly rising. Bisect some ferny woods. At 1.3 miles, trees grow so close to the cliffline it is challenging to get through. While hiking along this cliffline, look through the trees toward the tan sandstone massifs across the valley. In the near, spot occasional rock shelters in the cliffline. A keen eye will identify Indian Arch above a little before the trail curves right then ascends wooden stairs. Indian Arch will be found at the top of the stairs. This 25-foot reddish span is lower on one end than the other is but has a long classic arch look. You can easily walk under it—and atop it. Work your way up the left side of the arch as you face it, the uphill side. From atop the span it is an easy walk up to higher stone slabs away from the arch. Here, you can look out across the Gladie Creek and Red River hollows and beyond at the rock ramparts of the Red River Gorge. What a view and what an arch! On the backtrack, I bet you will see more alluring sights on this trek.

Mileages
0.0   Bison Way trailhead
0.4   Rock hop Sergeant Branch
0.5   Left on Sheltowee Trace
0.8   Bridge stream
1.1   Bridge stream
1.5   Indian Arch
3.0   Bison Way trailhead

CLIFTY WILDERNESS LOOP

Hike Summary: Explore the federally designated Clifty Wilderness using the Osborne Bend Trail, set on the north side of the Red River Gorge. This trek loops through the wilderness using remote high ridges surrounding Copperas Creek. At times, the path joins old settler and forest roadbeds as it rambles amid pines and oaks. The last part of the hike dips to Sal Branch, then meets KY 715, a road traveling along the Red River. From there, walk a little over

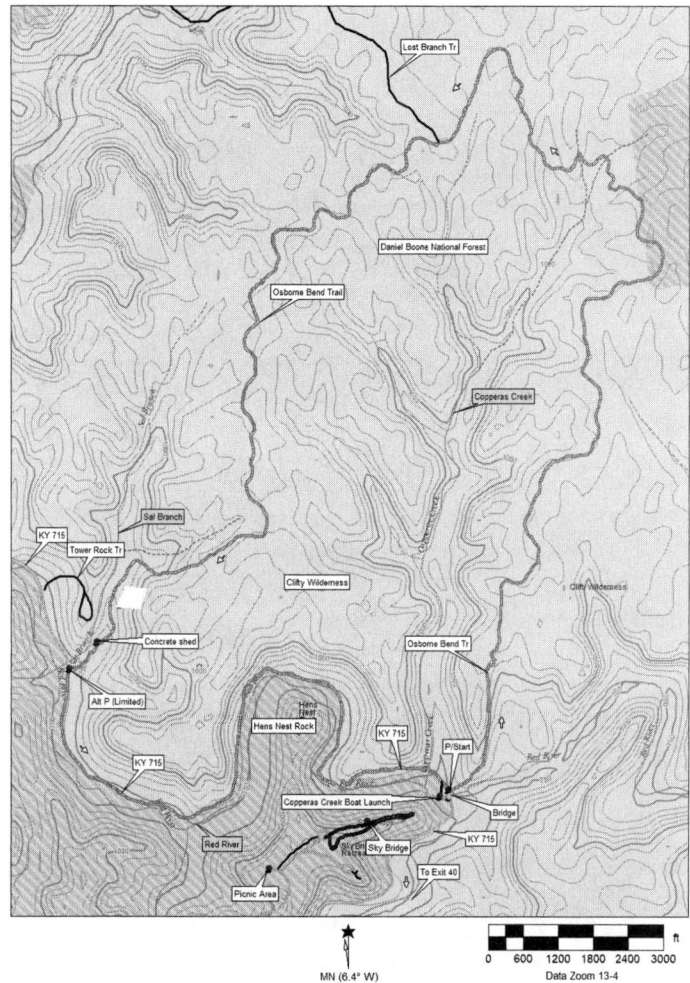

two miles through the gorge on the paved two-lane road, returning to the trailhead.

DISTANCE: 9.2-miles
HIKING TIME: 5 hours
DIFFICULTY: Difficult due to distance
HIGHLIGHTS: Wilderness
CAUTIONS: Potentially confusing old roads in wilderness
FEES/PERMITS: Permit required if camping in the Red River Gorge between 10 p.m. and 6 a.m.

OTHER TRAIL USERS: None
TRAIL CONTACTS: Cumberland Ranger District, 2375 KY 801 South, Morehead, KY 40351, (606) 784-6428, www.fs.usda.gov/dbnf

Finding the trailhead: From exit 40 on the Bert Combs Mountain Parkway, take KY 15/KY 715 north for .7 mile then turn right onto KY 715 north. Follow it for 4.9 miles, and veer right, staying with KY 715 as a road goes straight to Sky Bridge. Continue on KY 715 north for 1.4 more miles to reach the trailhead on the right, just after crossing the bridge over the Red River. GPS Trailhead Coordinates: N37° 49.209', W83° 34.480'

The Osborne Bend Trail is the longest path in the Clifty Wilderness, which occupies the eastern half of the Red River Gorge. Established in 1985, the untamed land encompasses 12,646 acres, and contain 15 sensitive, rare or endangered plants and more biodiversity. However, much of it was farmed and logged before becoming part of the National Natural Landmark that is the Red River Gorge. Today, the Clifty Wilderness and the Red River Gorge are considered scenic jewels of the Daniel Boone National Forest.

What is wilderness anyway? After eighteen-thousand-six-hundred pages of testimony and the consolidation of sixty-five bills, the Wilderness Act of 1964 was passed by Congress. The legal definition of wilderness, spelled out in the bill, is as follows: "A wilderness, in contrast with those areas where man and his works dominate the landscape, is hereby recognized as an area where the earth and its community of life are untrammeled by man, where man . . . is a visitor and does not remain." Ranging from six to over nine million acres in size, wilderness areas have multiple uses. Clifty Wilderness is known particularly for hiking, backpacking and climbing.

Leave the Red River trailhead just above Copperas Creek paddler launch. The Osborne Bend Trail immediately climbs, rambling along bluffs overlooking the Red River before turning away north. User-created spur trails leave to backcountry sites. Be watchful. Come alongside a cliffline at .3 mile then curve around a draw, still ascending. By .7 mile, you have achieved the ridgecrest, ascending around 400 feet. Now you are in typical upland woods of the Cumberland Plateau—pine, oak, holly black gum and sourwood. Deciduous magnolias are sprinkled in, too.

The trail remains gentle. At 1.7 miles, the Osborne Bend Trail splits left as an officially abandoned forest trail splits right, southeast. At 2.2 miles, the trail curves left to join old Copperas Ridge Road. At 2.5 miles, abruptly leave left from old Copperas Ridge Road. Luckily, the wilderness trails are signed at critical junctures like this one. The path becomes more primitive. It now begins a pattern of dipping into the uppermost drainages of Copperas Creek, then climbing out of them and then back to the next drainage. The path is working to stay within wilderness and national forest boundaries.

At 3.5 miles, the path curves south as it joins Osborne Bend Ridge. You are now out of the drainages, yet some parts of the old roadbed you are following are eroded. At 3.9 miles, reach a trail intersection. Here, the Lost Branch Trail descends to Gladie Creek then meets the Sheltowee Trace. Our hike stays with Osborne Bend Trail, making a pleasant woodland ramble above Sal Branch to the right and Copperas Branch to the left. Elevation change is minimal.

At 6.0 miles, the trail drops right as it enters a draw. Come along a cliffline and keep descending in thick rhododendron. At 6.3 miles, turn south, now above Sal Branch. Keep descending to reach a concrete shed, now in disuse. Pass a second concrete shed, then drop more to meet KY 715 at 6.8 miles. Parking is very limited here and not recommended. Turn left here, now following KY 715.

Truly, road walking is not the most desirable part of hiking, but find solace in the fact you are walking through the scenic Red River Gorge. Ahead, the road circles around Hen Rock, a stone protrusion across the Red River. As you continue, the rock pillar of which Sky Bridge is a part is visible above. Before too long you are rolling into the trailhead, passing the spur road down to the Copperas Creek paddler launch, ending the wilderness hike at 9.2 miles.

Mileages
0.0   KY 715 trailhead
2.2   Briefly join old Copperas Ridge Road
2.5   Abruptly leave left from old Copperas Ridge Road
3.5   Turn south, now on Osborne Bend Ridge
3.9   Lost Branch Trail leaves right
6.0   Drop off Osborne Bend Ridge
6.8   Left on KY 715
9.2   KY 715 trailhead

ANGEL WINDOWS WHISTLING ARCH SKY BRIDGE

Hike Summary: This adventure combines three short highlight filled hikes to geological features in the Red River Gorge. Located nearby one another, it is a simple matter to visit the delicate Angel Windows, then drive to the Whistling Arch trailhead, then hike to this rock span with a nearby view. The best is saved for last when you make the loop atop and beneath Sky Bridge, a massive arch complemented with views galore. Picnic facilities are near this final trailhead.

DISTANCE: .6-mile, .6 mile and .7 mile respectively
HIKING TIME: 1.2 hours
DIFFICULTY: Easy

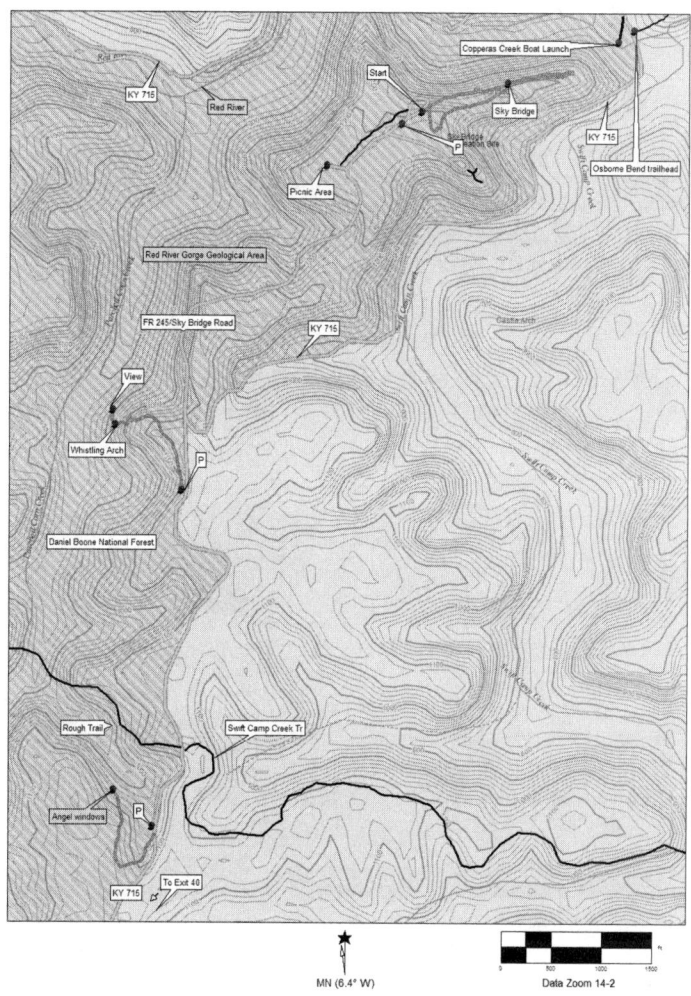

HIGHLIGHTS: Three vastly different arches, views
CAUTIONS: None
FEES/PERMITS: Permit required if camping in the Red River Gorge between 10 p.m. and 6 a.m.
OTHER TRAIL USERS: None
TRAIL CONTACTS: Cumberland Ranger District, 2375 KY 801 South, Morehead, KY 40351, (606) 784-6428, www.fs.usda.gov/dbnf

Finding the trailhead: From exit 40 on the Bert Combs Mountain Parkway, take KY 15/KY 715 north for .7 mile then turn right onto KY 715 north. Follow it for 4.0 miles to reach the Angel Windows

trailhead on your left. Next, continue on KY 715 for .8 mile farther to the Whistling Arch trailhead on your left. Finally, continue for .2 mile farther on KY 715, then stay straight, joining FR 245, Sky Bridge Road, and follow it for .8 mile to the parking area on your right before the turnaround loop road and Sky Bridge Trail. GPS Trailhead Coordinates: N37° 47.925′, W83° 35.470′

Visitors to the Red River Gorge commonly combine these three nature trails, since they are all short and in close proximity to one another. Do them in the order presented, since coming from the Mountain Parkway you will encounter them in that order. All the hikes are easy, so take your time and soak in the sights. The walk to Angel Windows circles around a hollow to reach a pair of small arches located next to one another at the end of a rock ridge. Whistling Arch is a single stone opening with a nearby rockhouse. Also, enjoy an outcrop and view into the Red River Gorge. Finally, you can utilize the picnic facilities before or after your loop walk at Sky Bridge. Here, head out a stony ridgeline walking atop Sky Bridge, enjoying multiple overlooks into the gorge before returning along the base of the cliffline with Sky Bridge towering above. What a lineup!

From the Angel Windows trailhead, join the signed trail going south on a rocky rooty path running parallel to KY 715. After a bit the path curves west, above a dark hollow where a tributary of Parched Corn Creek flows below. Turn back north and come alongside a cliffline. Here, check out the well-explored rockhouses just off the trail. After a little more than a quarter-mile come to the end of a rock outcropping and the Angel Windows. Here, stand two arches, with a common central column. The first window is low and bulky, under 4 feet in height, whereas the second window has a more delicate classic arch look to it and stands about 6 feet high with a tapering outer column. Walk through the arches and admire them from both sides before backtracking to the trailhead.

Now to Whistling Arch, .8-mile down KY 715. From this parking area you travel north on a pine shaded track with KY 715 to your right. The path veers northwest to a rib ridge and then you come to a towering stone massif below which is a big rockhouse to the right. If you walk into the rockhouse you will see the hole-like opening of Whistling Arch to your left. It is wider than is high, a rather low arch through which an adult has to duck for passage. After walking through Whistling Arch continue along the side of the stone tower above you then open onto a sandstone precipice. A view opens north across the vale of Parched Corn Creek toward the Red River.

After backtracking, continue to Sky Bridge Recreation Area, a signature highlight of the Red River Gorge, of which Sky Bridge is the centerpiece. Not only can you enjoy the loop trail of Sky Bridge, but also some roadside overlooks as well as shorter paths leading to still more vistas of the special slice of the Daniel Boone National Forest. From the parking area walk toward the circular auto turnaround and pick up the asphalt Sky Bridge Trail as it wanders along a narrow sandstone ridge. Views open to the left toward Red River and to the right into Swift Creek watershed. Scraggly shortleaf pines rise from the hardscrabble sandstone. Then at .2 mile you find yourself atop Sky Bridge. Walk directly over it. Keep along the ridge, enjoying more views, especially an overlook at .3 mile. The Red River isn't far below as you peer into the Clifty Wilderness across the waterway. Steps lead down to the base of the stone ridge where you have been walking. Return toward the trailhead along the base of a cliffline, then come to Sky Bridge again, now above you. Here, it resembles a classic high arch, a regal span of stone stretching across the heavens above. Also, note the small arch within an arch on the lower left side of Sky Bridge as you come to it.

Continue along the cliffline to reach 75 steps leading up a fissure in the rock. Once on top it is but a short distance to the trailhead, completing the final hike in this triumvirate of rewarding trails in the Red River Gorge.

Mileages
0.0   Angel Windows trailhead
0.3   Angel Windows
0.6   Angel Windows trailhead
0.0   Whistling Arch trailhead
0.3   Whistling Arch
0.6   Whistling Arch trailhead
0.0   Sky Bridge trailhead
0.2   Sky Bridge
0.3   View, descend to cliffline
0.7   Sky Bridge trailhead

ROCK BRIDGE ARCH CREATION FALLS TURTLE FALLS

Hike Summary: This popular, highlight-heavy hike explores rock and water features of upper Swift Camp Creek in the Red River Gorge. Leave the picnic area/trailhead, dropping past a dripping cliffline to reach Rockbridge Fork and Creation Falls. From there, be amazed by Rock Bridge Arch, a stone span stretching across Swift Camp Creek. Next, enter Clifty Wilderness, exploring the valley of Swift Camp Creek to view Turtle Falls, a slender spiller dropping off a cliffline into a stone alcove.

DISTANCE: 4.0-miles loop including spur
HIKING TIME: 2.2 hours
DIFFICULTY: Moderate
HIGHLIGHTS: Creation Falls, Rock Bridge Arch, Turtle Falls
FEES/PERMITS: Permit required if camping in the Red River Gorge between 10 p.m. and 6 a.m.
OTHER TRAIL USERS: None
TRAIL CONTACTS: Cumberland Ranger District, 2375 KY 801 South, Morehead, KY 40351, (606) 784-6428, www.fs.usda.gov/dbnf

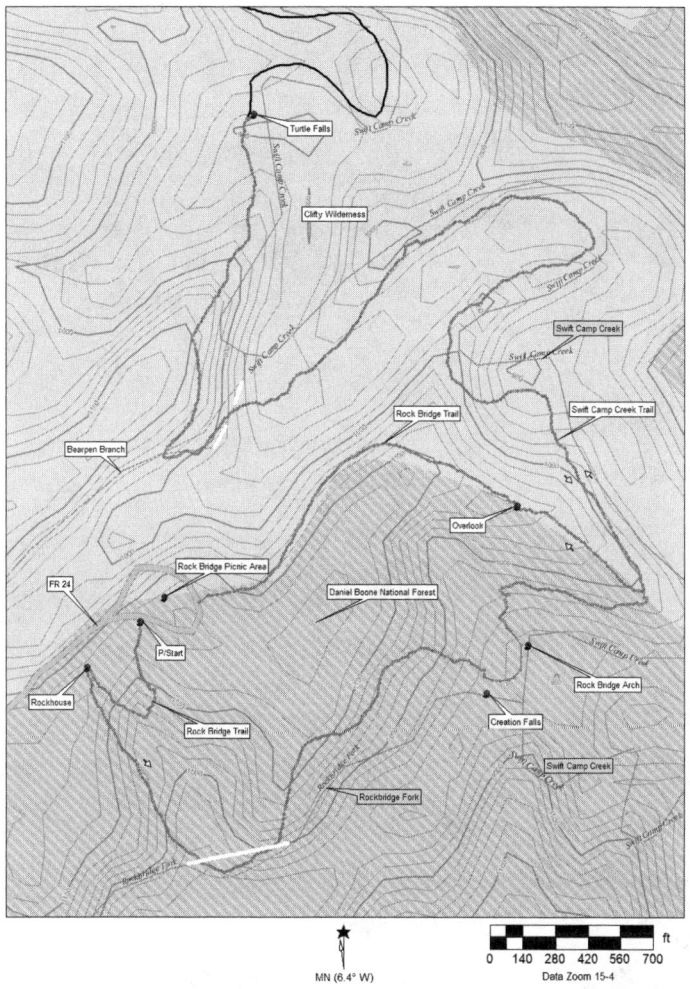

Finding the trailhead: From exit 40 on the Mountain Parkway near Pine Ridge, take KY 15 north for 1.3 miles to turn right on KY 715 north. Follow KY 715 north for .4 mile to turn right on Rock Bridge Road and follow it for 3.3 miles to dead end at the Rock Bridge Picnic Area. GPS Trailhead Coordinates: N37° 46.206', W83° 34.022'

The Rock Bridge Trail is a deservedly popular Red River Gorge destination. It makes a short loop from the picnic area at Rock Bridge Picnic Area to encounter geological and aquatic wonderments for which the Red

River Gorge is known. Our hike follows that basic and worthwhile loop but with a little side excursion into the adjoining Clifty Wilderness. Here, you will reconnoiter the picturesque Swift Camp Creek valley, with its big trees, lush vegetation, rock formations and alluring waterway featuring everywhere-you-look beauty to reach Turtle Falls. This easy to hear but somewhat difficult to reach cataract makes a 25-foot plunge from the cliffline of Swift Camp Creek into a colorful recess of rock. Turtle Falls also goes by the name of Turtleback Falls and Pooch Turtle Falls.

Name aside, the cataract makes a worthy exclamation point on this hike and additional reason to explore this part of the Clifty Wilderness. Your hike starts at the circular loop road of Rock Bridge Picnic Area, equipped with shaded picnic tables and a restroom. Leave south from the loop road on the Rock Bridge Trail, a path of old asphalt. Descend under oaks, sourwood and pines. Turn into a hollow, using steps to reach a huge, tall rockhouse with a very low flow, part time waterfall dripping from its heights. Turn down along a tributary of Rockbridge Fork under a mantle of white pine towering over a riot of vegetation.

At .4 mile, come alongside Rockbridge Fork and start down its hollow. By .7 mile, you are at 12-foot Creation Falls, the point where Rockbridge Fork—after flowing over a series of rock slabs—makes a white tumble first over a stone lip then angles down a widening rock slab, filling a massive pool bordered in rhododendron on one side and a sloped sand beach on the other side. Agile rock hoppers can cross Rockbridge Fork above the falls then walk downstream to access the sand beach, getting a face-on look at the cataract, located just upstream from where Rockbridge Fork gives its waters up to Swift Camp Creek. An easier to access elevated platform is just downtrail and requires no stream crossings. Creation Falls was named for nearby Rock Bridge Arch being an arch formed by water erosion.

The Rock Bridge Trail turns down Swift Camp Creek then at .5 mile you are at Rock Bridge Arch. And true to its name, the stone span completely extends across Swift Camp Creek, forming not only an arch but also a true bridge. Rock Bridge Arch stretches about 60 feet across the stream, about 8 feet high above the water and has a bridge-like form. The trail takes you directly beside the arch and also allows a look at the geological feature from both sides.

Continuing downstream, meet the Swift Camp Creek Trail at .9 mile. Join the natural surface Swift Camp Creek Trail for now, returning to this intersection later. Continue along Swift Camp Creek, rollercoastering along, stepping atop golden pine needles on the trailbed, flanked by evergreens. Stay along the rim of the gorge, gaining stream views. At

1.3 miles, the trail follows the stream while making a significant 180 degree bend. Yet the turn is so gradual a hiker would have to be watching the sun to know for sure of this directional change from northeast to southwest.

At 1.9 miles, the trail leads directly up Bearpen Branch, slicing through a mini-gorge with low but close stone walls before turning back out to the rim of Swift Camp Creek. Resume along this bigger stream then you hear Turtle Falls at 2.2 miles. You cannot miss it since the unnamed stream of Turtle Falls flows across the trail before tumbling off the rim below. Getting to the base of this falls can be difficult. Exercise caution. Hikers will be rewarded with a face-on view of this tributary diving 20 feet from an overhung rim, splattering onto a sandy landing pad below. Iron-stained rock walls form an eye-catching backdrop to Turtle Falls. The scene around the falls is classic Red River Gorge—Swift Camp Creek flowing in curves, stone walls rising from its banks, boulder jumbles and an overhanging rockhouse, all complemented with copious vegetation.

Backtrack from Turtle Falls, returning to the Rock Bridge Trail at 3.5 miles. Rejoin the nature trail as it climbs from Swift Camp Creek along a steep and narrow piney ridgeline. Pass a developed overlook at 3.7 miles, allowing looks into the Swift Camp Creek valley below. Note the numerous carved stone steps along the way. The path levels off before returning to the north side of the picnic area, and hike's end.

Mileages
0.0   Rock Bridge Picnic Area trailhead
0.4   Creation Falls
0.5   Rock Bridge Arch
0.9   Swift Camp Creek Trail
2.2   Turtle Falls
3.5   Rejoin Rock Bridge Trail
4.0   Rock Bridge Picnic Area trailhead

HIDDEN ARCH SILVERMINE ARCH

Hike Summary: This two-pronged hike takes you to two separate and very different natural arches in the south side of the Red River Gorge. Starting at the busy Koomer Ridge Campground, the hike wanders by some walk-in tent campsites before curving along Koomer Ridge to reach an overlook, then Hidden Arch, a small yet scenic geological feature. Loop back toward the trailhead to then pick up the Silvermine Arch Trail. Here, you traverse hilltops to

reach a sandstone ledge and another view before dropping to big, bulky Silvermine Arch, near a tributary of Chimney Top Creek.

DISTANCE: 4.5-miles
HIKING TIME: 2.3 hours
DIFFICULTY: Easy-moderate
HIGHLIGHTS: Views
CAUTIONS: None
FEES/PERMITS: Permit required if camping in the Red River Gorge between 10 p.m. and 6 a.m., does not apply to Koomer Ridge Campground, separate fee required for it
OTHER TRAIL USERS: None
TRAIL CONTACTS: Cumberland Ranger District, 2375 KY 801 South, Morehead, KY 40351, (606) 784-6428, www.fs.usda.gov/dbnf

Finding the trailhead: From Exit 33 on Bert Combs Mountain Parkway near Slade, take KY 15 South (it actually runs east) 5 miles to Koomer Ridge Campground, on your left. Enter the campground

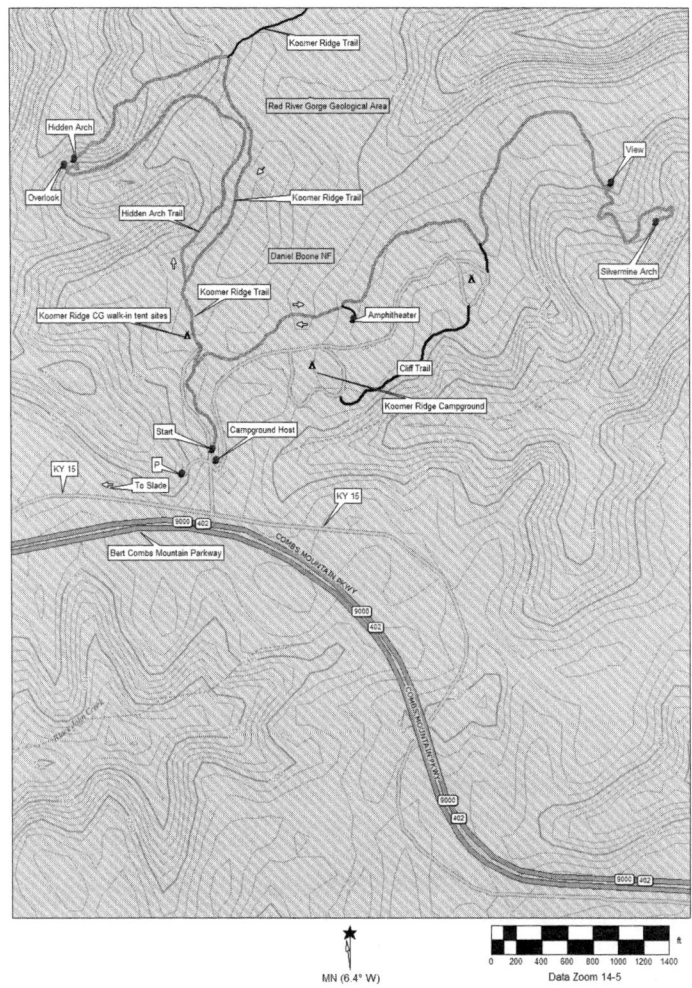

road and take the first left into the backpacker parking area. GPS Trailhead Coordinates: N37° 46.935', W83° 38.164'

This trek with four major highlights starts at a fun campground and excellent base camp for exploring the trails of Daniel Boone National Forest's Red River Gorge. Your first trip to Koomer Ridge Recreation Area can be a bit confusing, but if you follow this narrative you will look like an old pro! Furthermore, the trails here are well maintained and well signed, easing the challenge. From the backpacker parking area, walk east back toward the main road and just to the left, north, of the campground host, you will see sign indicating the Koomer Ridge Trail. Pick up this singletrack path on a piney ridge, northbound, divided by campground roads on both sides.

At .2 mile, reach an intersection. The Silvermine Arch Trail splits right. You will return here later. For now, stick with the Koomer Ridge Trail to immediately cross the walk-in campsite parking. The Koomer Ridge Trail cuts directly through the sites and into woods to reach another trail intersection at .3 mile. Here, split left onto the Hidden Arch Trail. It runs parallel to the Koomer Ridge Trail amid mountain laurel, oaks and pines. At .5 mile, the two paths nearly merge before the Hidden Arch Trail curves sharply left, westerly. At .9 mile, the Hidden Arch Trail turns past a short spur trail leading to a piney sandstone ledge where you can gaze into the valley of Right Fork Chimney Creek.

Beyond the overlook, the path cuts into a cleft in the ridge. Steps lead down to a rockhouse where to your right stands Hidden Arch, a low curving opening along the lower ledge. Hikers have traditionally climbed through the 4-foot opening, where you can look at it from both sides. Beyond here, the Hidden Arch Trail continues at the base of a cliffline, then works its way upward to meet the Koomer Ridge Trail at 1.2 miles. Turn right here, southbound, and make an easy walk atop wooded Koomer Ridge. At 1.6 miles, complete the loop portion of the hike and continue through the walk-in tent sites of the campground to turn left onto the Silvermine Arch Trail. The first part of this path wanders through the greater campground area, with spur paths leading to campsites. However, the correct route is clear.

Pass the short spur to the campground amphitheater at 2.0 miles. The walking is easy atop the forested ridge. Find yourself at another intersection at 2.3 miles. Here a short spur leads to the campground, but we stay left, heading for Silvermine Arch. Hike amid black gum, sourwood, oak and pine. At 2.7 miles, the Silvermine Arch Trail curves past a more expansive overlook in the Chimney Creek vale. The hike then drops straight off the ridge, descending 78 wooden stairs, a very long staircase. However, its gets you off the ridgetop and closer to Silvermine Arch.

Now wind through moister forest of magnolia, rhododendron and hemlock. At 2.9 miles, break through another cliffline and at 3.0 miles you are at Silvermine Arch. It is an uneven span, much higher on one end than the other, and many times larger than Hidden Arch. This water erosion arch is about 30 feet long, very dark and wet underneath. Nevertheless, you can walk all around it, below, it atop it and gain perspectives of the span from several vantages. Small rockhouses stand behind Silvermine Arch.

From here it is 1.5 miles back to the trailhead. For an optional return, you can walk the campground road and/or the Cliff Trail. Koomer Ridge Campground is a fine destination. The campground host keeps the facilities in good condition. The campground has a fully equipped bathhouse with hot showers. Toilets and water spigots are never far from your campsite. Each campsite includes picnic table, lantern post and leveled tent pad. Of special note are the walk-in tent campsites through which the first part of this hike travels. They are for those who want to get a little farther from the car, but not too far. The campground is open year-round, with the water cut off during winter.

Mileages
0.0   Koomer Ridge Trail near campground host site
0.2   Stay left with Koomer Ridge Trail
0.3   Left on Hidden Arch Trail
0.9   View then Hidden Arch
1.2   Right on Koomer Ridge Trail
1.6   Left on Silvermine Arch Trail
2.7   Overlook and long staircase
3.0   Silvermine Arch
4.5   Koomer Ridge Trail near campground host site

WHITTLETON ARCH

Hike Summary: This Sheltowee Trace hike starts near a popular campground at Natural Bridge State Park, then passes through the campground before reaching full-blown woods. From here, it heads up the beautiful Whittleton Creek Valley, leaving state park land to enter the Daniel Boone National Forest. The scenery continues improving until the Trace reaches the Whittleton Arch Trail, which leads to this massive stone feature.

DISTANCE: 3.0-mile there and back
HIKING TIME: 1.4 hours
DIFFICULTY: Moderate
HIGHLIGHTS: Whittleton Arch, low flow falls at arch
FEES/PERMITS: Permit required if camping in the Red River Gorge between 10 p.m. and 6 a.m.
OTHER TRAIL USERS: None
TRAIL CONTACTS: Cumberland Ranger District, 2375 KY 801 South, Morehead, KY 40351, (606) 784-6428, www.fs.usda.gov/dbnf

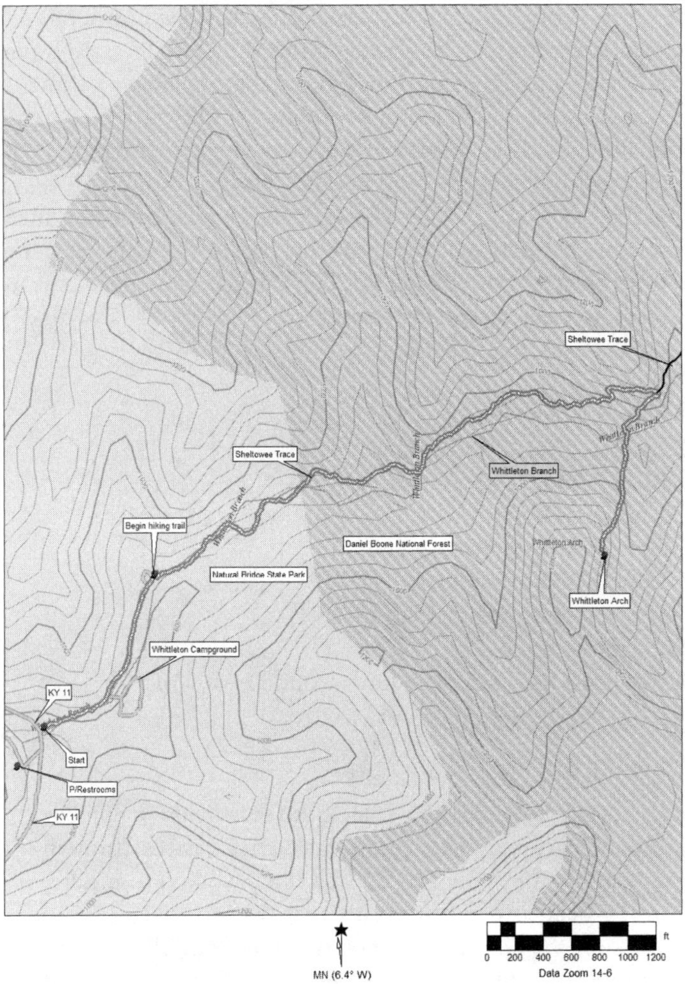

Finding the trailhead: From exit 33 on the Mountain Parkway near Slade, head south on KY 11 for 2.2 miles, passing the entrance to the Whittleton Campground at Natural Bridge State Park on your left. Just beyond the campground entrance road turn right and cross the Middle Fork Red River on a low water bridge to reach a parking area with restrooms. Do not park in Whittleton Campground then hike to the arch. GPS Trailhead Coordinates: N37° 46.788′, W83° 40.550′

Whittleton Arch | 47

The short hike to Whittleton Arch goes through several phases. It starts at the entrance to Whittleton Campground, one of the two camping areas at Natural Bridge State Park. You actually walk through the campground, perhaps inspecting the sites for future overnighting possibilities. Next join the Sheltowee Trace on a footpath traversing gorgeous Whittleton Creek valley, centered with a clear meandering stream over which you cross using quaint wooden bridges. Overhead, white pines form a superstory above lesser hardwoods and evergreens. Of course, ubiquitous outcroppings of stone add a geological touch to the whole affair. The next phase is the entering of the side canyon where Whittleton Arch is found. Here, you walk along a lesser stream then dead end at an imposing semicircular stone theater. Upon coming closer you see the light opening of Whittleton Arch then hear the drip of the falls dropping from Whittleton Arch, a rewarding sight.

From the parking area, walk the low water bridge over Middle Fork Red River then carefully cross KY 11 to enter Whittleton Campground. Open seasonally, Whittleton Campground offers water, campsites with or without electricity and hot showers, set along Whittleton Branch. Pass directly by the campground entrance station and follow the blacktop campground road along Whittleton Creek. Campsites spur off the road you are following deeper into the hollow of Whittleton Creek. At .3 mile, leave the campground, passing an informational signboard and picking up the singletrack Sheltowee Trace. The stream flows to your left.

The Sheltowee Trace follows a narrow gauge railroad bed—the Mountain Central Railway—that ran through here in the late 1800s, part of a logging operation linking the Natural Bridge area to Chimney Top. The rail line is hard to imagine now—today the Trace is a singletrack path in a lush forest. However, you can clearly delineate the railroad bed's course. The Sheltowee Trace goes off and on this railroad bed. The Whittleton Branch valley is quite lovely—white pines tower overhead dropping golden needles on the trailbed. Wooded hills broken by rock bluffs stand sentinel above and rise steeply beyond Whittleton Branch. This very clear stream, protected by cabin sized boulders, gurgles over small rocks below the trail.

The Eastern hemlock, an evergreen tree, is a mainstay tree of eastern Kentucky's cool, moist valleys such as Whittleton Branch. The conical crown of horizontal branches, emanating from a reddish-brown trunk, often droops to the ground. However, in thickets such as here along Whittleton Branch, lower branches are absent of needles or absent altogether. When growing in stands, the fallen needles create an acidic soil that cuts down on understory vegetation. Look on the underside of the small needles for a whitish band running the length of the needle. Pioneers made brooms from the branches, and the bark was used as an agent to tan leather. Hemlocks range on the Cumberland Plateau and Southern Appalachians from northern Alabama through eastern Kentucky, then become more widespread in the northern states, from Wisconsin to Maine. This tree is under threat by the non-native insect known as the hemlock wooly adelgid. The future of the hemlock stands such as these is in serious doubt and when the hemlocks die, the forest composition will be altered.

Soon span Whittleton Branch by footbridge twice, leaving the state park to enter national forest land at .6 mile. At 1.1 miles, leave the old railroad grade that once ran through a jumbled boulder garden ahead. The path splits left and climbs farther up the valley, avoiding the boulder jumble. Intersect the Whittleton Arch Trail at 1.2 miles. Turn right here, descending to and crossing Whittleton Branch on a footbridge. The stream can be dry here, upstream of the aforementioned boulder jumble.

The Whittleton Arch Trail squeezes up a rhododendron-filled hollow, crossing the small streamlet flowing from the hollow. Ferns and wildflowers thrive here in season. At 1.5 miles, reach a rock cathedral and the big, wide Whittleton Arch. This is one of the biggest arches by mass in the Red River Gorge and is very wide, too, and seems more of a rockhouse. In wetter times, a waterfall pours from atop the arch, rolling down the stone then diving 25 feet to the ground below, but can slow to a trickle and is rarely flowing boldly. The rock, water and forest form a primeval setting at the arch, shining as one more example of the natural beauty found within Kentucky's Daniel Boone National Forest.

Mileages
0.0   Whittleton Campground entrance road at KY 11
0.3   Leave campground
1.2   Right on Whittleton Arch Trail
1.5   Whittleton Arch
3.0   Whittleton Campground entrance road at KY 11

NATURAL BRIDGE LOOP

Hike Summary: This loop travels to and through some of Natural Bridge State Park's most exciting features, including the park's namesake Natural Bridge. First, climb past Balanced Rock, an unusual geological feature. Top out near Natural Bridge. Descend past a gazebo then check out massive Natural Bridge from above and below, also tackling Fatmans Squeeze. From there climb the Needles Eye Stairway to a panorama from Lovers Leap. Pass another rewarding view of Natural Bridge from afar then return to the arch one more time before descending back to the trailhead on the historic Original Trail.

DISTANCE: 3.2 miles
HIKING TIME: 1.7 hours
DIFFICULTY: Moderate, lots of ups and downs
HIGHLIGHTS: Balanced Rock, Natural Bridge, Lovers Leap, views

CAUTIONS: Numerous trail intersections, pets not permitted
FEES/PERMITS: None
OTHER TRAIL USERS: None
TRAIL CONTACTS: Natural Bridge State Resort Park, 2135 Natural Bridge Rd., Slade, KY 40376, (606) 663-2214, www.parks.ky.gov/parks/resortparks/natural-bridge/

Finding the trailhead: From exit 33 on the Mountain Parkway near Slade, head south on KY 11 for 2.5 miles to turn right onto the

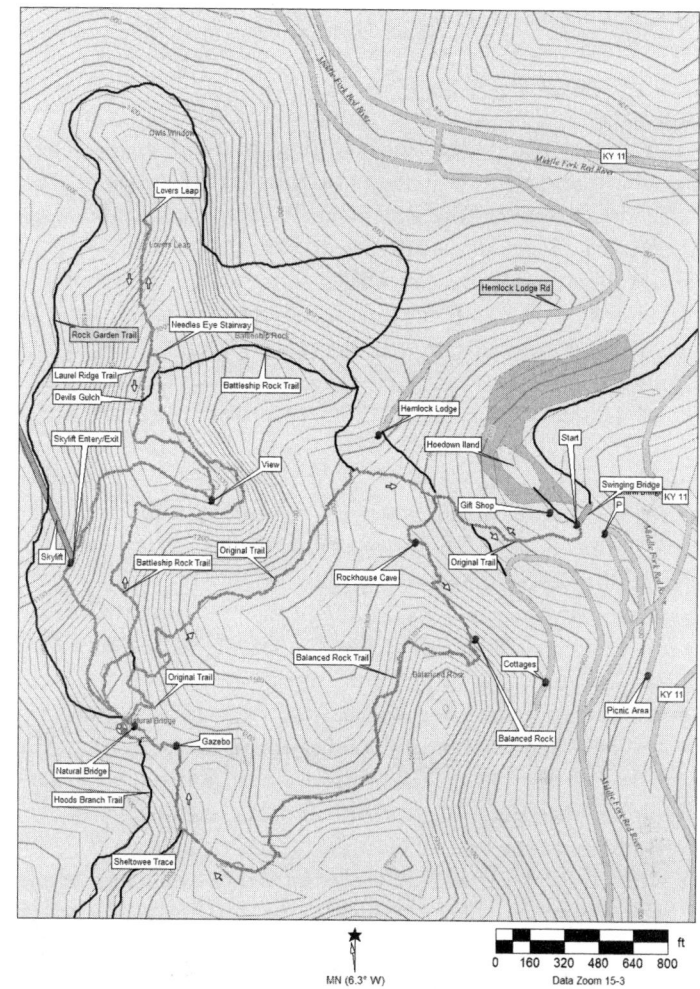

road indicating "Activities Center and Trails." Turn right onto the road then cross Middle Fork Kentucky River then take an immediate right. The hike starts near the swinging bridge over the river. GPS Trailhead Coordinates: N37° 46.538', W83° 40.689'

This is one of the best hikes in the entire state of Kentucky. And that shows in its popularity. Therefore, I recommend avoiding obviously busy times to make this trek at Natural Bridge State Park, nice weekends, holidays, etc. However, do make the hike. Natural Bridge is surrounded by the Daniel Boone National Forest and that is why hikes here are included in this guide.

The hike leaves the state park activities center trailhead near the swinging bridge and the gift shop. Join the Original Trail and climb. Pass a spur to the park cabins then reach a flat area at .2 mile. Here stand a trail signboard and benches. Ahead is your return route, the Original Trail. Head left here on the Balanced Rock Trail. Climb many stone steps then come alongside a cliffline and barred Rockhouse Cave. Climb more stairs then come to Balanced Rock at .4 mile. The stone illusion is not two rocks with one balanced on top of the other but a single rock with an inverted middle that will one day topple, yielding to time and the elements.

Beyond Balanced Rock the climbing resumes before the trail reaches a pine/oak ridgeline with views to the south. You have climbed almost 400 feet. At .6 mile, come to a flat rock used as a seat by weary hikers. Meander the ridgetop, heading west. At .8 mile, reach an intersection. Here, the Sand Gap Trail/Sheltowee Trace leaves left, but we turn right on our hike and descend to a saddle then climb an open rock slab, come near a gazebo then reach the Natural Bridge at .9 mile. Go ahead and walk out the Natural Bridge for a view from the level deck of the massive arch. Backtrack just a bit and take the stairway heading under the arch. First, you must negotiate Fat Man's Squeeze, which is truly a slender passageway between the Natural Bridge and a boulder. When the trails are busy lines form on each side of the squeeze waiting for hikers to get through, since hikers cannot pass one another within the squeeze.

Then you are at the base of Natural Bridge, standing 65 feet high and 78 feet wide. Its form is classic arch and almost looks sculpted. After admiring the arch from different angles, resume the hike by walking under the arch and hanging a left on the Battleship Rock Trail. Hike in the shadow of massive sandstone palisades. Stay with the Battleship Rock Trail, passing a spur to the Original Trail. Keep along rockhouses, clifflines and stonewalls.

Come to a trail intersection at 1.5 miles. Here, take the steep Needles Eye Stairway, circling along an immense stone edifice. Ascend stone carved steps to make Laurel Ridge Trail at 1.6 miles. Turn right here, heading toward Lovers Leap on a level piney track. Soon reach Lovers Leap. Look north toward the Red River Gorge and down at KY 11, as well as a stone pillar in the near known as Owls Window. Backtrack along the Laurel Ridge Trail, passing the intersection with the Needles Eye Stairway and Devils Gulch Trail. At 2.0 miles, open onto an immense flat stone slab delivering fantastic panoramas. Look over at the enormous Natural

Bridge. People walking atop it look like ants. The park lake, Hoedown Island, and other facilities lie below. Continue the ridgetop walk among black gum, red maples and shortleaf pines. Pass the park skylift entry/exit at 2.2 miles. Enjoy the view here, down to lower Hood Branch and the Middle Fork Kentucky River.

The trail may become crowded at this point, as skylift hikers walk to Natural Bridge, which is reached at 2.4 miles. Cross the stone span then pass under it again via Fatmans Squeeze. Pass under the arch a second time then join the historic Original Trail, approaching a century old. This path takes you down past little rain shelters and along a creeklet that flows into a cave. Stay right at an intersection with the Battleship Rock Trail and soon you have completed the loop. A short .2 mile backtrack returns you to the trailhead.

Mileages
0.0   Trailhead near swinging bridge and gift shop
0.2   Left on Balanced Rock Trail
0.4   Balanced Rock
0.9   Natural Bridge
1.6   Lovers Leap
2.0   View
2.4   Natural Bridge
3.2   Trailhead near swinging bridge and gift shop

SAND GAP LOOP

Hike Summary: This long loop explores the quiet side of Natural Bridge State Park. Most of the walk wanders through Natural Bridge State Park Nature Preserve. First circle around Lower Hood Branch before making Sand Gap and a lonely ridge. Views await here in the high country before joining the Sheltowee Trace and visiting venerable Natural Bridge and a brief encounter with the crowds, then just as quickly leave them behind on the Hood Branch Trail. Circle around a wildflower rich vale as you skirt rock palisades, finally returning to the trailhead.

DISTANCE: 10.0 mile loop
HIKING TIME: 5.5 hours
DIFFICULTY: Difficult due to distance
HIGHLIGHTS: Solitude, Natural Bridge, wildflowers

CAUTIONS: Hike has no bailout options first 7.1 miles
FEES/PERMITS: None
OTHER TRAIL USERS: None
TRAIL CONTACTS: Natural Bridge State Resort Park, 2135 Natural Bridge Rd., Slade, KY 40376, (606) 663-2214, www.parks.ky.gov/parks/resortparks/natural-bridge/

Finding the trailhead: From exit 33 on the Mountain Parkway near Slade, head south on KY 11 for 2.0 miles then turn right into the Natural Bridge State Park entrance indicating, lodge, dining,

Sand Gap Loop | 55

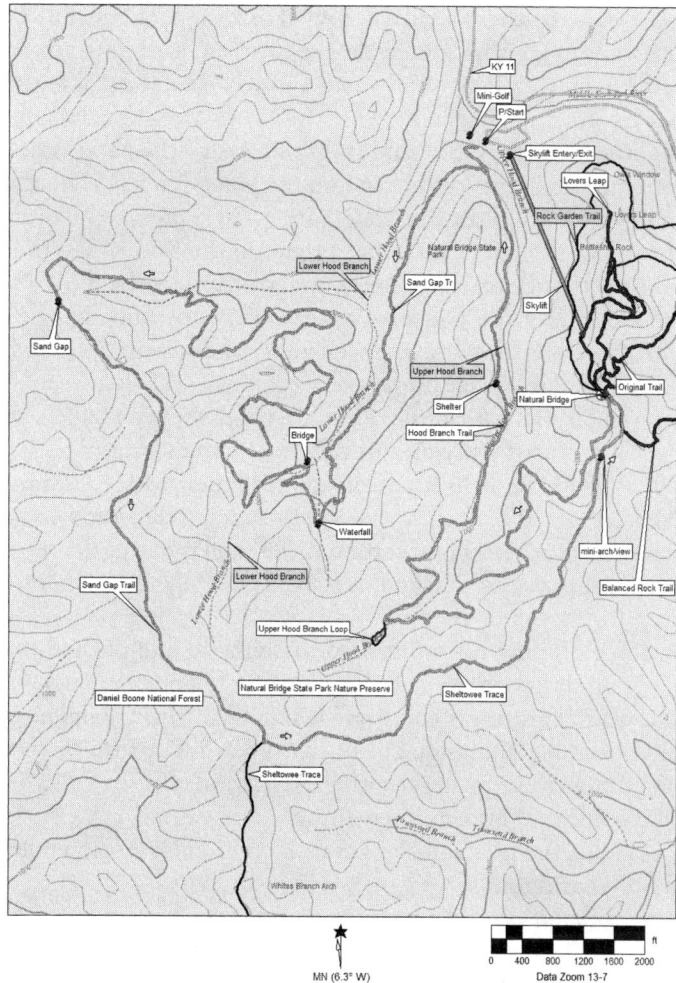

skylift. Cross the bridge over the Middle Fork Red River then immediately turn right toward skylift and mini-golf. Follow the park road to dead end near the restrooms and mini-golf area. GPS Trailhead Coordinates: N37° 46.891′, W83° 41.465′

When other trails at Natural Bridge and the Red River Gorge are hopping, I guarantee you solitude on the Sand Gap Trail. This lesser-used and underappreciated path presents scenic beauty as well as an opportunity to enjoy nature on nature's terms. The reason for its lesser use is once you commit to the trail, it is a full 7.1 miles before you intersect any other trails that will return you to civilization. So most people just skip it. Don't make this same mistake. Instead, prepare yourself, then tackle the Sand Gap Loop with gusto and you'll be rewarded with wild Kentucky scenery throughout.

The hike has a most un-wild trailhead. Leave the parking area near the restrooms and mini-golf, then join the Hood Branch Trail and enter the 1,188-acre Natural Bridge State Park Nature Preserve. Climb along on old roadbed then at .1 mile, head right on the Sand Gap Trail. Signs warn of the distance and time for hikers to complete the loop. The path has a much fainter trailbed than other paths here. Start up the Lower Hood Branch watershed, staying well above the stream. Pine and beech trees grow tall here. Bridge numerous feeder branches on a steep hillside.

At 1.3 miles, the path curves around a tributary just above a five-foot waterfall. This can run dry by autumn. At 1.6 miles, cross a hiker bridge over Lower Hood Branch. It is worth noting that the Hood Branch watershed is one of the healthiest, cleanest streams in Kentucky, as proven by its rich macroinvertebrate communities, and is one of the reasons for the nature preserve, established in 1981. The refuge is also home to the rare Virginia big-eared bat.

Continue circling the watershed, weaving in and out of drainages, defying your ability to predict where it is going next, even with GPS, map, compass, tarot cards and a rabbit's foot. At times, wind near stone precipices, coming alongside clifflines. At 2.8 miles, turn under a rock overhang from which issues a spring. At 3.7 miles, bridge a large tributary of Lower Hood Branch, then climb up its valley. At 3.9 miles, just before reaching the ridgeline, look for a large circular erosion hole in the cliffline to your right.

Come to Sand Gap at 4.0 miles. A side trail leads right to private property. The Sand Gap Trail turns southeast in sandstone and pines, undulating on the ridgeline. At first, the ridge is quite narrow, then widens and becomes dominated by hardwoods. Note where signs indicate national forest land. The ridge itself forms the boundary between the nature preserve and the national forest. Watch for the remains of an old pond before coming to the trail intersection with the Sheltowee Trace at 5.6 miles. Stay left here, as the Sheltowee Trace and the Sand Gap Trail run in conjunction. The walking is easy here. At 7.0 miles, the trail reaches a sandstone knob where steps have been carved into the stone. Just before this, look for a small mini-arch in the rock near your feet. Climbing a bit on the knob, open to views to the southeast.

Reach a trail intersection at 7.1 miles. You are now entering the busy part of the park but are rewarded with a trip to Natural Bridge. Turn left here, quickly passing a gazebo and coming to Natural Bridge. Walk atop the sandstone span, 75 feet wide and 68 feet high, enjoying panoramas all around. Backtrack then descend by steps and through Fatmans Squeeze. This opening between boulders is so narrow as to prevent two hikers from passing one another at the same time.

Check out the Natural Bridge from below, admiring its curved lines, then join the Hood Branch Trail, leaving the crowds behind. Vegetation is thick along the trail, even where it travels along clifflines. Bridge small Upper Hood Branch at 8.6 miles. Here a short loop circles the uppermost stream and is good for wildflowers in season. Turn down Upper Hood Branch, working around a few tributaries and criss-crossing Hood Branch. The walking becomes easier when it picks up an old roadbed. Come to a trailside shelter at 9.4 miles. Pass the intersection with the Sand Gap Trail at 9.9 miles and backtrack just a short distance to complete the loop. In the summertime the mini golf course should be open but you may be too tired to play!

Mileages

0.0	Trailhead near mini golf
0.1	Right on Sand Gap Trail
1.3	Five foot waterfall
2.8	Rock overhang with spring
4.0	Sand Gap
5.6	Left on Sheltowee Trace
7.1	Left to Natural Bridge
7.2	Left on Hood Branch Trail
8.6	Bridge upper Hood Branch
9.4	Trailside shelter
10.0	Trailhead near mini golf

Central Daniel Boone National Forest

ALCORN BRANCH FALLS

Hike Summary: Want to visit a seldom seen part of the Daniel Boone National Forest? If you do, head to the forgotten community of Arvel and take the Sheltowee Trace to Alcorn Branch Falls, a 30-foot seasonal spiller, flowing at its best from late fall through spring. The hike is easy as you follow an old roadbed from Arvel on the Sheltowee Trace, then the trail descends as a singletrack path to a semicircular rockhouse into which Alcorn Branch spills. If you want to add on to the hike, consider continuing on the Sheltowee Trace to meet War Fork.

DISTANCE: 1.6-mile there-and-back
HIKING TIME: 1.0 hours
DIFFICULTY: Easy
HIGHLIGHTS: Alcorn Branch Falls, spring
CAUTIONS: Be very careful accessing Alcorn Branch Falls
FEES/PERMITS: No fees or permits required
OTHER TRAIL USERS: None
TRAIL CONTACTS: Daniel Boone National Forest, London Ranger District, 761 South Laurel Road London, KY 40744, (606) 864-4163, www.fs.usda.gov/dbnf

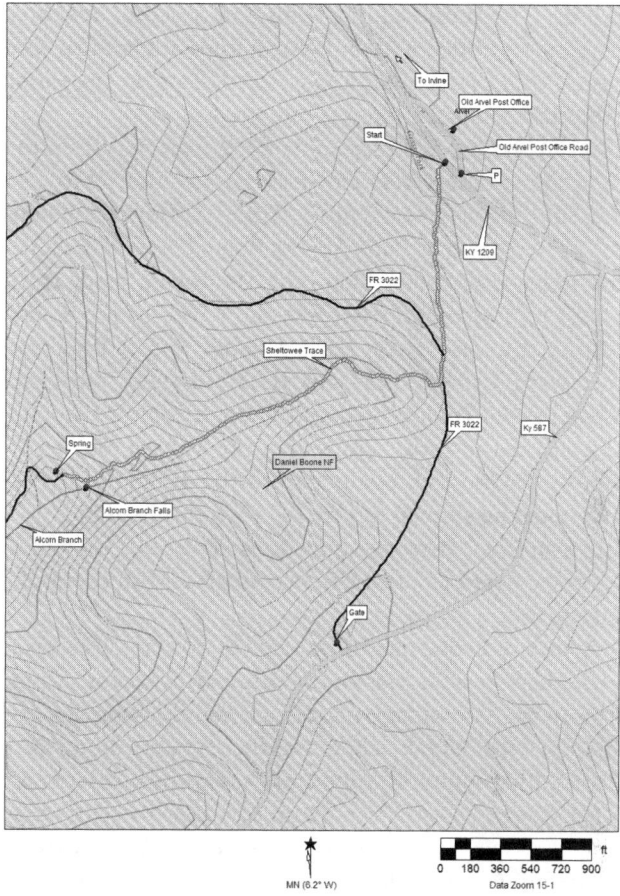

Finding the trailhead: From the town square in Irvine, take KY 89 south/KY 52 west for a short distance before KY 89 splits. Stay with KY 89 south for 7.2 miles to meet KY 1209. Turn left and follow KY 1209 for 13 miles to the Sheltowee Trace, leaving south from KY 1209, just bit east of the old Arvel post office. Park at the eastern intersection of KY 1209 and Old Arvel Post Office Road. There is room for one car. If you reach KY 587 beyond Old Arvel Post Office Road you have gone .1 mile too far. GPS Trailhead Coordinates: N37° 31.058', W83° 53.121'

This is one of those adventures that hikers always mean to do but can't seem to get there. The hike to Alcorn Falls isn't cool or famous. The hike isn't long. The trailhead is distant and obscure. Yet those who do make it here are rewarded with not only a fine cataract in a lesser visited parcel of the Daniel Boone National Forest but also the satisfaction of trekking the trail less trod.

Look for the Sheltowee Trace sign on KY 1209. Head south on a doubletrack and immediately veer left, passing a memorial to local fan and user of the Sheltowee Trace, Embry Curry. Follow an abandoned dirt road south, once known as Polly Sparks Road, bordered by fence on both sides, amid fields and woods. Here, the Sheltowee Trace is following a right-of-way. Quintessential rural Kentucky rolls in the distance.

At .2 mile, the Sheltowee Trace reaches Forest Road 3022. Here, briefly head left on the doubletrack then cut right onto a singletrack path. The Sheltowee Trace now winds under full-blown woods. Look for white oaks beside the path. White oaks are known for their longevity. Interestingly, oaks are technically part of the beech family. White oaks grow throughout the state of Kentucky, with the greater Ohio River valley offering near ideal growing conditions. The range of white oak covers most of the eastern US, from Texas north to Minnesota, then east to Maine and south to Florida.

The high quality wood has been prized by Americans for generations. Among other uses it once was made into barrel staves, bringing about the all but forgotten nickname barrel oak. Wildlife may love white oaks more than man does. Woodpeckers and turkeys are among the birds that enjoy the nuts. Raccoons and chipmunks savor the nutrient packed treat, too. Deer eat the acorns and browse on tender white oak twigs.

The headwaters of Alcorn Branch flow in the hollow to your left. If you hear it gurgling over rocks the falls will be flowing well. The stream is starting to cut a gorge. At .7 mile, come alongside the upper part of Alcorn Branch Falls then curve away on the edge of a chasm. At this point you can carefully look into the semicircular overhanging basin into which Alcorn Branch dives 30 feet, bespattering broken rock. Ahead—if the water is up—a side stream makes an additional waterfall dropping into the alcove.

Once at the bottom you can circle behind the cataract, admiring the spiller from all angles. But getting there can be tough. Use caution. To access the falls from the trail requires walking near and perhaps over the side stream falls—not a good idea. Most hikers continue on, passing an overhanging bluff with a spring below it, in which lie some old barrels and a sign placed by the Forest Service not to drink the water. Keep going a bit farther then make your way to Alcorn Branch then walk upstream to the falls.

Lower Alcorn Branch is also worth exploring, using the Sheltowee Trace. When the water is up you will pass a second side stream waterfall, but if the water is down, even Alcorn Branch will run underground on its way to War Fork. The Sheltowee Trace does cross Alcorn Branch once before reaching War Fork. It is 1.4 miles from Alcorn Branch Falls to the confluence of Alcorn Branch and War Fork. If continuing along War Fork, you will find a remote, little visited valley, much like Alcorn Branch. Despite lesser use, this section of the Sheltowee Trace is in generally good shape. Try it.

Mileages
0.0   KY 1209 trailhead
0.2   FR 3022
0.8   Alcorn Branch Falls
1.6   KY 1209 trailhead

TURKEY FOOT LOOP

Hike Summary: This woodsy circuit hike originates at fine, fun and free Turkey Foot Campground, on the banks of the stream War Fork. You first cruise the War Far Creek Valley then climb to a remote ridge before dipping to the Hughes Fork streamshed, then walk along its lower reaches, passing Turkey Foot Cascades before returning to the campground. A cutoff trail makes a shorter loop possible. Elevation changes between high and low points are around 400 feet.

DISTANCE: 4.1-mile loop
HIKING TIME: 1.8 hours
DIFFICULTY: Easy-moderate
HIGHLIGHTS: Waterfall, solitude
CAUTIONS: None
FEES/PERMITS: No fees or permits required
OTHER TRAIL USERS: None
TRAIL CONTACTS: Daniel Boone National Forest, London Ranger District, 761 South Laurel Road London, KY 40744, (606) 864-4163, www.fs.usda.gov/dbnf

Finding the trailhead: From Exit 76 on I-75 near Berea, head east on US 421 18 miles to McKee. Once in McKee, turn left on KY 89, passing through the town square. Follow KY 89 North 3 miles to a

sharp, signed right turn onto paved Forest Service Road 17, Macedonia Road. Follow Macedonia Road for 0.5 mile, turning left onto a paved road that becomes FR 4, Turkey Foot Road after 1 mile. Continue forward on gravel FR 4 two more miles to Forest Road 345. Turn left onto FR 345, and follow it 0.2 mile to the right turn into Turkey Foot Campground, crossing a low water bridge. Stay

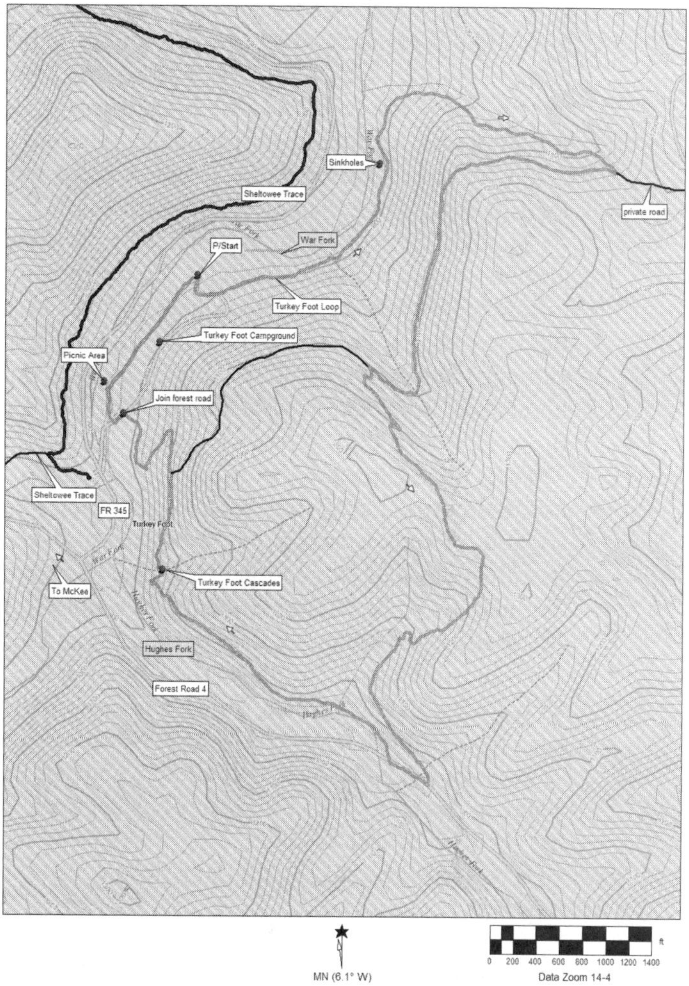

Turkey Foot Loop | 65

left on the recreation area road when it makes a loop and park at the far lower end of the loop, near a small field, beyond the picnic area. GPS Trailhead Coordinates: N37° 28.237′, W83° 54.873′

Turkey Foot Recreation Area, situated along the banks of War Fork, is a nifty little part of the Daniel Boone National Forest. Located near the town of McKee, the underused destination features a streamside picnic area and a pleasant shaded campground at which I have stayed many a night. Anglers take note; War Fork is stocked with trout during the colder part of the year and bass inhabit the stream year-round. And to top off the recreation possibilities a fun loop trail with a waterfall circles through adjacent national forest land. A shortcut path in the loop allows for circuit hike of a little over 2 or 4 miles.

Finding the start of the trail can be tricky your first time. From the parking area at the small field on the north end of the recreation area, follow the recreation area loop road right and uphill. Do not cross the field and pick up a user-created trail going along War Fork. Walk 300 feet along the loop road then split left onto a signed singletrack hiking trail in hemlocks. Hike along a bluff above War Fork. Watery seeps flow across the trail.

At .5 mile, enter an area of sinkholes—the War Fork valley has a complicated plumbing system, with sinks, seeps, springs and underground streams, including parts of War Fork that flow underground much of the year. Just ahead, a signed turn takes the loop right, easterly, staying on national forest land. The trail turns up a hollow, passing a low cliffline. At 1.0 mile, the loop trail rises to uplands and nears private land. Here, a private road goes forward but the loop cuts back acutely right, joining an old logging grade. Make an easy level cruise under tall hardwoods. Partial views open across the War Fork valley. At 1.2 miles, the trail bisects a cut in the hillside, where a former logging rail passed through. Though this area was timbered, it has been a long while and the forest has regrown in lush fashion.

The trail then curves around a hollow full of straight trunked tulip trees. At 1.7 miles, reach an easily missed trail intersection. Here, the logging grade keeps straight and forms the shorter loop here. However, our longer loop splits acutely left and uphill as a narrow footpath in ferny woods. Climb a little less than 200 feet in .3 mile, then level off. Stay straight as the trail crosses an old grassy road. Down we go at 2.2 miles, dipping toward Hughes Fork.

Step over a streambed just before emerging onto Forest Road 4 at 2.7 miles. Turn right and follow the gravel road for .1 mile, then split right onto the signed path just before the forest road bridges Hughes Fork. Here, the trail rejoins the old logging grade running above clear Hughes Fork. The evenly spaced uneven ground reveals where the old railroad ties were located. At 3.3 miles, the trail splits left away from the railroad grade. At this point, the route doesn't seem to make sense until you come alongside a seasonal stream and 12-foot waterfall, Turkey Foot Cascades. The trail runs just above the lip of the cataract as makes a two-stage curtain drop from a rock rim. Hikers have to scramble a bit to get a face on look at the spiller, which can run dry in autumn.

The trail returns to the old railroad grade at 3.4 miles. At 3.5 miles, intersect the other end of the short loop. Keep straight, then switchback downhill toward the campground. Reach the campground road near campsite #1 at 3.8 miles. The campground itself is open from mid-April through mid-November and features tent pads, picnic table, fire ring and lantern post in quiet, scenic woodland. As mentioned, camping is free. From here, join the campground road left then cruise past the picnic area, completing the hike at 4.1 miles.

Mileages
0.0   Parking area on FR 345
0.5   Sinkholes
1.0   Acute right
1.7   Left at trail intersection
2.7   FR 4
3.3   Turkey Foot Falls
3.8   Campground road
4.1   Parking area on FR 345

RESURGENCE CAVE

Hike Summary: From the trailhead at Turkey Foot Recreation Area, take Kentucky's master path —the Sheltowee Trace—along the slopes of the War Fork valley to Resurgence Cave, a stony maw from which War Fork emerges after its underground meanderings. Along the way, look for previous signs of habitation, when subsistence farmers eked out a life here in what is now the Daniel Boone National Forest. Afterwards, consider enjoying other activities at Turkey Foot, such as picnicking, fishing, swimming or camping.

DISTANCE: 4.8-mile there-and-back
HIKING TIME: 2.2 hours
DIFFICULTY: Easy-moderate
HIGHLIGHTS: Resurgence Cave, homesites
CAUTIONS: None
FEES/PERMITS: No fees or permits required
OTHER TRAIL USERS: None
TRAIL CONTACTS: Daniel Boone National Forest, London Ranger District, 761 South Laurel Road London, KY 40744, (606) 864-4163, www.fs.usda.gov/dbnf

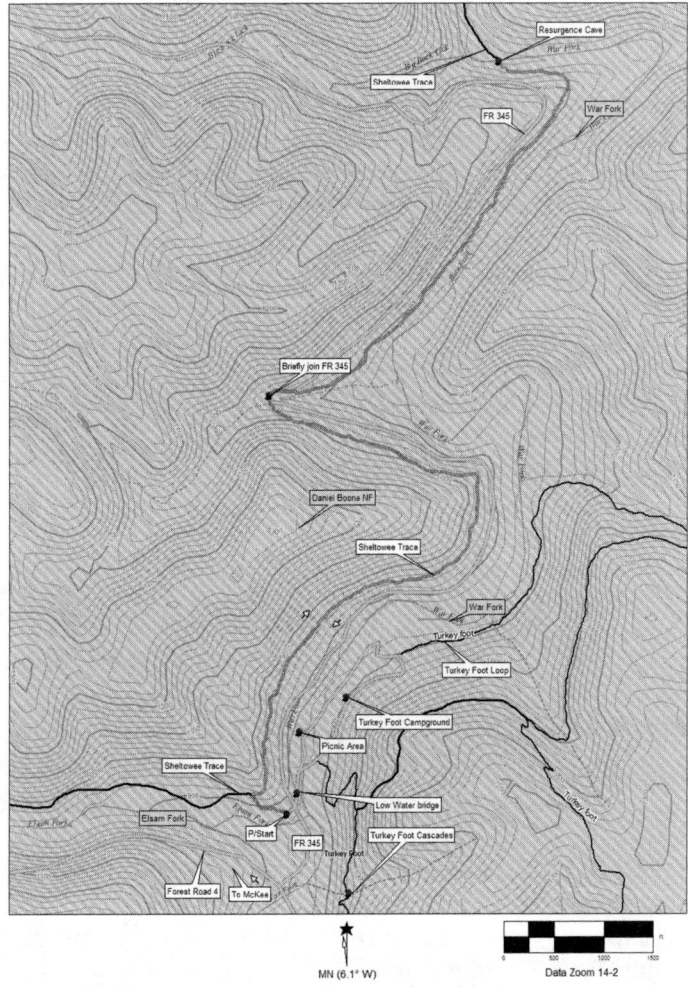

Finding the trailhead: From Exit 76 on I-75 near Berea, head east on US 421 18 miles to McKee. Once in McKee, turn left on KY 89, passing through the town square. Follow KY 89 North 3 miles to a sharp, signed right turn onto paved Forest Service Road 17, Macedonia Road. Follow Macedonia Road for 0.5 mile, turning left onto a paved road that becomes Forest Road 4, Turkey Foot Road, after 1 mile. Continue forward on gravel FR 4 two more miles to Forest Road 345. Turn left onto FR 345, and follow it 0.2 mile

to the right turn into Turkey Foot Campground. The hike starts here, on the left, near the crossing of a low water bridge of Elsam Fork and before the low water bridge crossing War Fork. There is parking room for 3-4 cars here. GPS Trailhead Coordinates: N37° 27.961′, W83° 55.065′

This hike is on Kentucky's top ten all time names list—you start at a place called Turkey Foot, then walk along War Fork to a place known as Resurgence Cave, all on the Sheltowee Trace. This portion of the Sheltowee Trace does parallel Forest Road 345 much of the way, but is not a distraction. In fact, it can be a positive. You can walk the Sheltowee Trace from Turkey Foot Recreation Area, then return on the trail you just walked, or on Forest Road 345. There is still another return route for the intrepid and daring—directly up War Fork. And this can only be done when War Fork is running underground—which it normally does from summer through fall, before remerging at Resurgence Cave. Then you can literally walk up the fascinating dried up streambed. The rocks can still be slick during then, however.

To start the hike from Turkey Foot Recreation Area, pick up the Sheltowee Trace access trail between the low water bridge crossing Elsam Fork and the low water bridge entering Turkey Foot Campground. The blazed path leads uphill to the Sheltowee Trace and a junction at .1 mile. Turn right here onto the Trace, heading up War Fork Valley on a single-track path. Note the different allowed usages for the Sheltowee Trace at this point. From here, going left, south, the section of the Sheltowee Trace to S-Tree Campground is open to ATVs; however, heading right, northbound, where our hike leads, it is only open to hikers. Moreover, the trail tread shows the difference usages.

The Trace soon saddles alongside rock bluffs split by rocky drainages cutting between them. Oak, maple, hickory and red bud are among the other species found in this forest. At this point, Forest Road 345 runs between the Trace and War Fork. The walking is easy along this level bench, a flat far above War Fork. At .5 mile, piled rocks indicate former farmland. Whoever cultivated this land also appreciated the relatively level terrain in this rugged country, where hardscrabble subsistence agriculture was the order of days past. Subsistence farmers, such as those who settled this locale, lived isolated lives of independence in the "land of do without."

It is no surprise this land has reverted to a vast forest, for which it is best suited. More rock piles appear at .8 mile. It seems improbable that this now lush Kentucky forestland was once cultivated, but it was. At .9 mile, the Sheltowee Trace curves sharply west, with War Fork. At 1.4 miles, the Trace joins Forest Road 345 around a curve to the northeast. Just beyond this curve, the Sheltowee Trace leaves the forest road right, easterly, and heads downhill toward War Fork. The Sheltowee Trace is now between FR 345 and War Fork, descending to a rock rim above War Fork, where you can look below at the normally visible rocks of the streambed—and a possible return route. The valley wall steepens, forcing the ST to twist away from War Fork among the trees on an uneven foot bed.

At 2.3 miles, the Trace intersects a wide old roadbed. To the left, uphill, the doubletrack leads up to Forest Road 345, which turns away from War Fork at this point. The Sheltowee Trace crosses the old roadbed, then descends to reach War Fork at 2.4 miles. Resurgence Cave is to your left. The Trace crosses the normally dry creek to reach a hemlock flat located on the far side of War Fork and makes for a good picnic spot and turnaround spot.

Resurgence Cave borders the west side of War Fork. Here, water emerges from a black void in a rock bluff into the War Fork streambed, boldly flowing and creating a pool, then continuing downstream. War

Fork runs belowground between Turkey Foot Recreation Area and Resurgence Cave. After examining the area you can then decide whether to backtrack on the trail, the forest road or up the War Fork streambed.

Mileages
0.0   Turkey Foot Recreation Area
1.4   Briefly join FR 345
2.4   Resurgence Cave
4.8   Turkey Foot Recreation Area

HAWK CREEK SUSPENSION BRIDGE AND FALLS

Hike Summary: This lesser done DBNF adventure uses Kentucky's master path—the Sheltowee Trace—to visit the scenic Hawk Creek valley. From the trailhead, the Trace winds north, cutting down the valley of a tributary of Hawk Creek. Along the way pass smaller falls and rockhouses before turning along gorgeous Hawk Creek. A wooden suspension bridge leads across the trouty watercourse to a streamside flat, ideal for camping or relaxing. However, the siren song of nearby Suspension Bridge Falls lures you to see this long, tall spiller drip into a boulder jumble, capping off the trek.

DISTANCE: 3.4-mile there-and-back
HIKING TIME: 2.0 hours
DIFFICULTY: Moderate
HIGHLIGHTS: Hawk Creek suspension bridge, Suspension Bridge Falls
CAUTIONS: Irregular terrain near Suspension Bridge Falls
FEES/PERMITS: No fees or permits required
OTHER TRAIL USERS: None
TRAIL CONTACTS: Daniel Boone National Forest, London Ranger District, 761 South Laurel Road London, KY 40744, (606) 864-4163, www.fs.usda.gov/dbnf

Finding the trailhead: Exit 41 on I-75 near London, take KY 80 west for .7 mile to KY 1956. Turn right onto KY 1956 west and follow it for 7.0 miles to the signed trailhead, on the right. GPS Trailhead Coordinates: N37° 9.766′, W84° 14.421′

This Sheltowee Trace hike leads down to a streamside environment where nature has been left to thrive. The superlatively attractive Hawk

Hawk Creek Suspension Bridge and Falls | 73

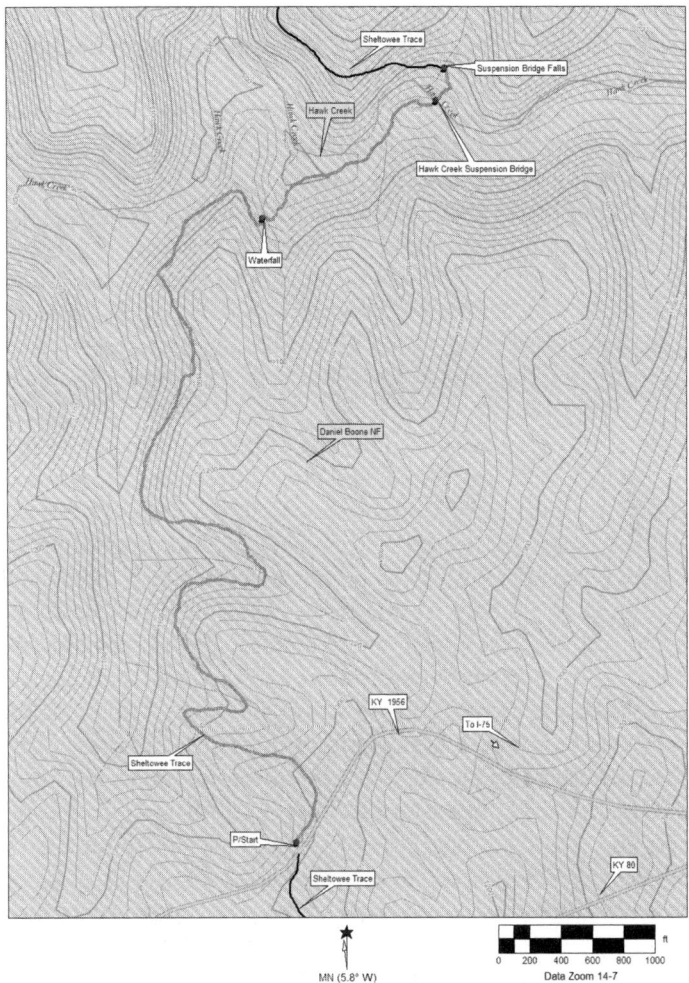

Creek Valley is the setting, where myriad rock formations rise from a rich forest and a pretty stream that the Trace spans on a suspension bridge. A waterfall is within earshot of the suspension bridge and a nearby flat makes for a good picnic spot. Moreover, consider this hike as an excellent, quick and scenic one night backpacking trip.

Start this hike by leaving north from KY 1956 on the singletrack Sheltowee Trace. The path curves below a residence, skirting the Daniel Boone National Forest boundary. Gray-trunked oaks, maples and hickories shade the Trace as it travels a sandy, sometimes root-strewn path.

Plastic white diamonds mark the Sheltowee Trace. Slope off the ridgeline and pick up an old roadbed that leads into dark evergreen thickets mixed with magnolia. The Trace curves past a small streamlet at .6 mile. The Trace leaves the roadbed beyond the streamlet and turns into a south facing slope where pines and chestnut oaks predominate, separating from the creek flowing well below. At 1.1 miles, the trail comes along the first major rock bluff and begins running beneath the richly wooded rim with Hawk Creek gurgling below and sandstone palisades rising overhead.

Descend by switchbacks between rock walls, suddenly turning east. Here you reach a feeder branch flowing over naked rock, forming a waterfall during wetter times. This falls spills about 12 feet in a curtain type straight drop, but can become but a drip at times. Rhododendron chokes the valley below.

The Sheltowee Trace runs along the cliffline of Hawk Creek in rugged basin of hemlock, beech trees and black birch trees. Occasional rockhouses rise overhead. Black birch is also known as sweet birch. When crushed, the twigs and leaves of this tree emit an aromatic odor. The oil of sweet birch, also known as oil of wintergreen, flavored candy and medicine in days gone by. Young trees, richer in the oil, were favored for use, but oil of wintergreen is now obtained from wood alcohol and salicylic acid, leaving such trees to thrive in the Daniel Boone National Forest. The dark brown-blackish bark of the black birch is somewhat shiny and has horizontal lines running through it. However, in larger trees the bark becomes plated. Black birch is found in moist valleys and north facing ridgelines in Eastern Kentucky south to Alabama and up to New England. The oval toothed leaves, 3-5 inches in length, turn yellow in autumn.

The Trace works upstream along Hawk Creek, flowing over shoals and slowing in deep dark pools. Gravel bars border the stream in spots. At 1.6 miles, the Sheltowee Trace leads past a massive old growth hemlock that will hopefully be preserved for future generations and not fall to the exotic pest known as the hemlock wooly adelgid that is decimating America's hemlock trees. Open onto an inviting flat with a campsite before reaching the wooden suspension bridge over Hawk Creek at 1.7 miles.

Take a look upstream and downstream from the suspension bridge. This bridge is just wide enough for a hiker with a full backpack. Hawk Creek, swaddled in thick vegetation, flows west toward its mother stream the Rockcastle River. A second campsite lies in the hemlock copse just on the far side of this bridge. From this point hikers can relax at the flat, save for one thing—the splashing sounds of nearby Suspension Bridge Falls are beckoning. The nearby cascade—formed by a tributary of Hawk

Creek—is emanating from a huge rock overhang fronted by a boulder jumble of the first order.

Stay on the ST just a short distance and you come to the creek of Suspension Bridge Falls. You can follow the creek upstream among boulders along a cliffline to reach the 36-foot spiller, dropping off an overhung rock rim into a boulder jumble. Work your way behind the cataract. You can also look down at Suspension Bridge Falls from a little hill in front of the falls, but neither vista point is easy to reach, though is worth the view.

After viewing the falls return to the hemlock copse by the suspension bridge. The copse is cool even on hot days. If you want to explore further northbound, the Sheltowee Trace stays on national forest land for two more miles before coming to a road walk segment.

Mileages
0.0   KY 1956 trailhead
0.6   Step over tributary
1.1   Waterfall
1.6   Big hemlock, flat
1.7   Hawk Creek suspension bridge, Suspension Bridge Falls
3.4   KY 1956 trailhead

Southern Daniel Boone National Forest

ROCKCASTLE NARROWS EAST LOOP

Hike Summary: The rewarding scenery on this adventure begins before ever leaving your vehicle, as you pass a pair of small arches en route to the trailhead on Forest Road 119. Once on the trail, hikers join the Rockcastle Narrows East Trail then the Sheltowee Trace to make Vanhook Cascade and Vanhook Falls. From there, turn down the scenic Cane Creek Valley, passing a lesser cataract to reach the Rockcastle River, a Kentucky wild river. Hike past the famed rapid known as The Narrows then walk up the geologically enthralling Rockcastle valley. Make a final climb from the river back to the trailhead, completing the circuit.

DISTANCE: 6.6-mile loop
HIKING TIME: 3.2 hours
DIFFICULTY: Moderate
HIGHLIGHTS: Vanhook Cascade, Vanhook Falls, Kentucky wild river
CAUTIONS: A few faint trail sections
FEES/PERMITS: No fees or permits required
OTHER TRAIL USERS: A few mountain bikers
TRAIL CONTACTS: Daniel Boone National Forest, London Ranger District, 761 South Laurel Road London, KY 40744, (606) 864-4163, www.fs.usda.gov/dbnf

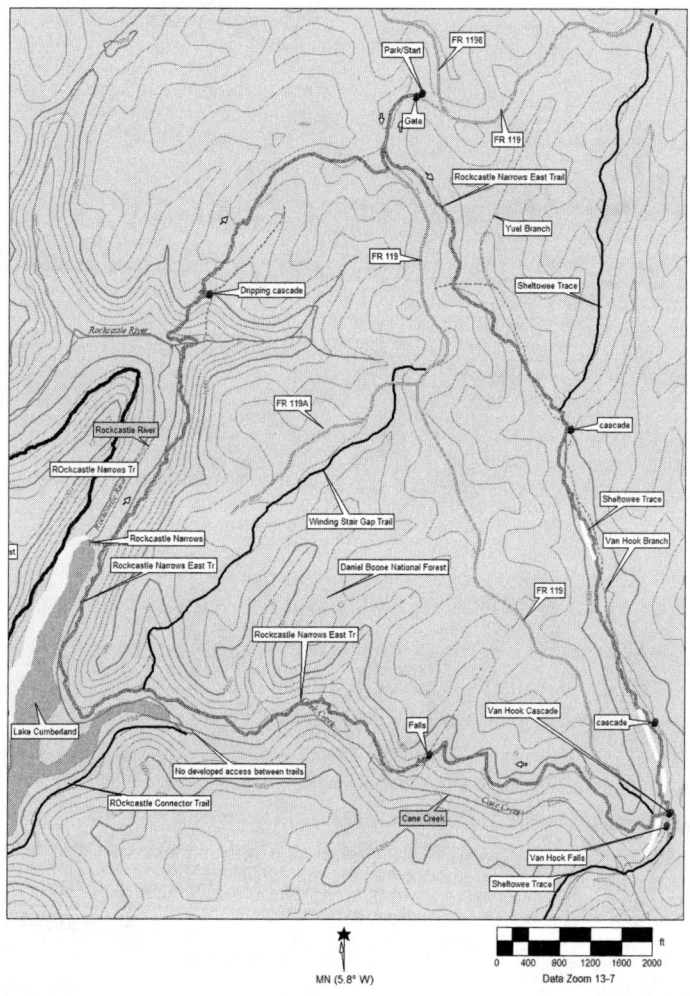

Finding the trailhead: From exit 38 on I-75 near London, head west on KY 192 for 5.7 miles and turn right onto paved Line Creek Road. Follow Line Creek Road for 2.7 miles then veer left onto gravel Forest Road 56. After 1.8 miles, veer left onto FR Forest Road 119 (away from New Hope Baptist Church). After 3.2 miles, stay left with FR 119 as FR 457 goes right and uphill. Continue for 2.1 miles more miles on FR 119, parking at the intersection of FR 119 and FR 1198. Park in the gravel to the right of the road, just after Forest Road 1198 goes right. GPS Trailhead Coordinates: N37° 2.977′, W84° 17.506′

The highlights are plentiful on this lesser visited circuit hike, in a remote segment of the Daniel Boone National Forest. Begin the hike by continuing up Forest Road 119, passing around a pole gate, southbound. Walk along the gravel track for .2 mile, then reach a signed trail junction. Here, head left on the singletrack Rockcastle Narrows East Trail under oak, maple, and holly. At .9 mile, step over Yuel Branch, shaded by impressive sized hemlocks. At 1.1 miles, meet the Sheltowee Trace, Kentucky's master path. Turn right here, southbound on the ST and cross Yuel Branch again, this time just above a 5 foot ledge drop cascade.

Keep down the valley, now following Vanhook Branch, flowing far below. At 1.9 miles, you are now along Vanhook Branch where a 7-foot horseshoe shaped waterfall spills into a rhododendron shrouded, waterworn stone cavity. Come to a trail intersection at 2.2 miles. For now, head left toward Vanhook Falls on the Sheltowee Trace, though you will return here later. Dip to Vanhook Branch, crossing it just above Vanhook Cascade, a 10-foot angled slide fall. Beyond here, the Sheltowee Trace circles above the rim of Vanhook Falls, reaching a stairway and wooden deck at an observation point of Vanhook Falls at 2.3 miles. Here, Vanhook Branch makes a wide curtain-like descent into a huge rock amphitheater, echoing the spill. Visitors can walk to and under the 35-foot high, 15 feet wide curtain of white.

Backtrack .2 mile from Vanhook Falls, leaving the Sheltowee Trace, westbound on the Rockcastle Narrows East Trail. Soon pass a spur leading uphill and to the right toward the end of FR 119. The Rockcastle Narrows East Trail turns down Cane Creek, into which Vanhook Branch flows. Curve in and out of evergreen rich hollows well above Cane Creek and around piney hillocks. At 3.3 miles, start dropping and pass a low-flow falls spilling down a slide 6 feet then diving 16 more feet from a ledge into a rocky defile bordered in rhododendron. The sound will alert you to it. Just ahead the trail takes you across the same stream at a short ledge drop.

Descend to come alongside Cane Creek. White pines are prevalent in the valley as you roller coaster through thick woods and boulders. At 4.2 miles, the easy-to-miss, faint Winding Stair Gap Trail leaves right up a hollow. In this area also, the Rockcastle Connector Trail—with no developed connection—leads from the south side of Cane Creek to Bee Rock Campground.

Our hike turns north into the perceptibly wider Rockcastle River valley at 4.4 miles. The river is likely backed up at this point as Lake Cumberland and appropriately quiet. Wind among incredible boulders, thick woods. Ferns thrive and moss grows on anything that doesn't move. By 4.8 miles reach the Rockcastle Narrows. Here, the Rockcastle River becomes pinched in and forces its way through a boulder garden. Quite a thrilling ride for whitewater enthusiasts who tackle "The Nars."

Enjoy more scenery affirming the status of the Rockcastle as a Kentucky wild river. At 5.4 miles, the Rockcastle turns west above a rapid. The trail makes its way around a muddy hollow. Be watchful here as trail users have made multiple paths working around the muddy hollow. Cross the stream of the hollow and briefly continue west along the Rockcastle River. At 5.5 miles, the easily missed correct path rises right away from the water while a user-created trail continues along the river bottom.

Make a steep climb away from the Rockcastle. Pass a low flow, dripping cascade near a cliffline at 5.7 miles. Keep working up by switchbacks.

At 6.1 miles, join a closed forest road accessing a wildlife clearing. Enjoy the easy grassy track after your 400-foot ascent. At 6.4 miles, come to Forest Road 119. Turn left here, northward, passing the other end of the loop on which you started. From there it is a simple .2 mile backtrack to the trailhead.

Mileages

0.0	FR 119 trailhead
0.2	Left on Rockcastle Narrows East Trail
1.1	Right on Sheltowee Trace
2.2	Left toward Vanhook Falls
2.4	Vanhook Falls, backtrack
4.2	Intersect faint Winding Stair Gap Trail
4.8	Reach The Narrows
5.5	Right turn away from Rockcastle River
6.4	Left on FR 119
6.6	FR 119 trailhead

CANE CREEK VIA BALD ROCK PICNIC AREA

Hike Summary: This hike starts at a fine picnic area and former fire tower site. It first uses the Sugar Tree Hollow Trail to link to Cane Creek Trail. Here, trace attractive Cane Creek in towering woods and thickets of rhododendron to dead end at a campsite and a forest road. The out and back trek affords solitude and wildflower viewing opportunities.

DISTANCE: 5.3-mile balloon loop
HIKING TIME: 2.8 hours
DIFFICULTY: Moderate
HIGHLIGHTS: Wildflowers, solitude
CAUTIONS: None
FEES/PERMITS: No fees or permits required
OTHER TRAIL USERS: None
TRAIL CONTACTS: Daniel Boone National Forest, London Ranger District, 761 South Laurel Road London, KY 40744, (606) 864-4163, www.fs.usda.gov/dbnf

Finding the trailhead: From exit 38 on I-75 near Corbin, take KY 192 west for 9.6 miles Bald Rock Picnic Area, on your right. GPS Trailhead Coordinates: N37° 1.984', W84° 13.364'

The Daniel Boone National Forest, established in 1937, covers over 700,000 acres in Kentucky. That is a lot of trees! In order to help protect the assets of the national forest, forest personnel established a series of fire towers to watch for conflagrations, to be manned during the fall and spring fire seasons and other times when fire danger was high, such as times of drought.

Where this hike starts, Bald Rock Picnic Area, was the site of a lookout tower, one of fourteen that were established in the national forest. The Bald Rock fire tower was in operation from the late 1930s until 1970, when the Daniel Boone National Forest moved to fire watching by airplane. The towers were then dismantled.

The Bald Rock tower site was turned into a picnic area. An information sign is located at the tower site, inside the picnic area's auto turn-

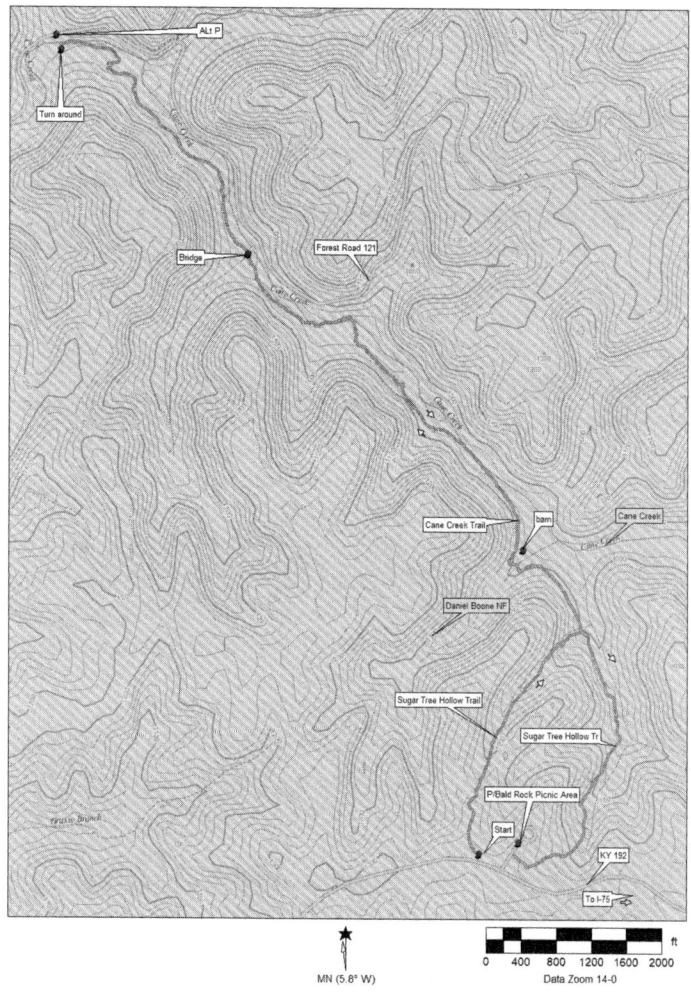

around. Bald Rock Picnic Area offers several picnic tables set in sun and shade, as well as restrooms and a sand volleyball court, plus horseshoe pits. The locale is open year-round. For us hikers it is also trailhead for the Sugar Hollow Trail, our conduit to explore the hills and hollows of Cane Creek, a tributary of the Rockcastle River. Nearly all of the Cane Creek drainage lies within the Daniel Boone National Forest, making it an important stream for forest flora and fauna. This part of Cane Creek is known for spring wildflowers. The lower part of the stream flows through Cane Creek Wildlife Management Area. The lowermost 6.6 miles of Cane Creek are annually stocked with trout.

Since the hike requires no major fords it can be done year-round, though spring for wildflowers and fall for colors are best. Winter will give you additional looks into trailside geology.

Finding the trailhead can be confusing. The Sugar Tree Hollow Trail, a loop trail, has two starting points. With KY 192 to your back, look left beyond the horseshoe pits for the westerly signed beginning of the Sugar Tree Hollow Trail, near KY 192. Join the singletrack path in oaks. It isn't long before you are dipping into a hollow and clifflines develop. The deeper you go into this north facing hollow the more favorable the situation for wildflowers such as trillium and wild ginger. The name Sugar Tree comes from the former practice of tapping the sap of maple trees for making sugar and syrup. Though commonly associated with New England, the tapping of maples took place throughout the mountain South.

Come alongside a trickling branch before reaching a trail intersection at .6 mile. Here, head left onto the Cane Creek Trail, stepping over the small creek you have been paralleling. Enter a wider hollow, yet as thickly wooded, with plants and trees growing in profusion. Continue down the hollow, where a field can be seen below. This field is part of a private inholding that also includes an old house and a barn. The Cane Creek Trail skirts the private property, staying on national forest land.

At .9 mile, step over a stream flowing in from your left. You are still circling around the private inholding. Just ahead, stay left with the blazed trail as a spur trail goes right to a barn. Keep in the woods, leaving the field and private property for good at 1.0 mile. The trail is running close to Cane Creek here, moving slow as this part of the 15-foot wide stream is sometimes dammed by beavers.

Enjoy traipsing down along the rhododendron-bordered watercourse, flowing over flat rock slabs, complemented by big boulders. At 1.2 miles, the trail and stream briefly pull apart. At 1.6 miles, Forest Road 121 runs along the creek, though you might not even know it is there unless the sounds of vehicle traffic drift into your ears. Thick woods make the road difficult to see even when the leaves are off the trees.

At 1.9 miles, the path uses a wooden hiker bridge to span a tributary stream. Ahead, look along Cane Creek as the stream flows under an overhanging rock ledge. Keep descending along the creek at a very moderate descent. At 2.6 miles open onto a campsite and the end of the trail. Here, Forest Road 121 stands across the creek, with no bridge afforded the hiker.

Since this is an out and back endeavor we don't need to ford Cane Creek. Instead, simply backtrack 2 miles up Cane Creek, returning to the intersection with the Sugar Tree Hollow Trail at 4.6 miles. Here, stay left, now ascending an evergreen-rich hollow where moss covers the tree trunks and boulders. Make the only significant climb of the hike as the hollow narrows. Then at 5.3 miles, the Sugar Tree Hollow Trail emerges on the grassy lower reaches of the picnic area, ending the hike.

Mileages
0.0   Bald Rock Picnic Area trailhead
0.6   Cane Creek Trail
2.6   FR 121, backtrack
4.6   Left on Sugar Tree Hollow Trail
5.3   Bald Rock Picnic Area trailhead

BEE ROCK LOOP

Hike Summary: This rewarding hike starts at a national forest campground of the same name. The hike crosses a historic bridge over the Rockcastle River then climbs to a vista from Bee Rock. Beyond there, the circuit surmounts a ridge then drops to the Rockcastle River. It then follows this designated Kentucky Wild River past The Narrows in gorgeous riverside woods amidst geological wonderment of cliffs, boulders and before returning to its origin.

DISTANCE: 5.6-mile loop
HIKING TIME: 2.5 hours
DIFFICULTY: Moderate
HIGHLIGHTS: Vista, bluffs, hiking along Kentucky wild river
CAUTIONS: None
FEES/PERMITS: No fees or permits required
OTHER TRAIL USERS: A few mountain bikers
TRAIL CONTACTS: Daniel Boone National Forest, London Ranger District, 761 South Laurel Road London, KY 40744, (606) 864-4163, www.fs.usda.gov/dbnf

Finding the trailhead: From Exit 38 on I-75 near London, head west on KY 192 18 miles to the bridge over the Rockcastle River. Turn right into Bee Rock Campground on Forest Road 624, the south side of the Rockcastle River, before crossing the river bridge. Follow FR 624 for .4 mile to the Sublimity Bridge on the left. GPS Trailhead Coordinates: N37° 1.676', W84° 19.294'

Bee Rock Recreation Area is a hotbed of outdoor fun, with camping, picnicking, fishing, paddling, motor boating and of course hiking. Vacationers have been coming to Bee Rock for over two hundred years to get

away from it all. In the early 1800s, Sublimity Spring Resort Hotel was located where the campground now lies. Columbus Graham, a hero in the War of 1812, ran the resort, which offered an escape from malaria, yellow fever, and other plagues of the lower South. It was described as "an Eden for children, a sanitarium for invalids, a paradise for lovers, and a haven of rest for the tired."

Bee Rock Loop | 87

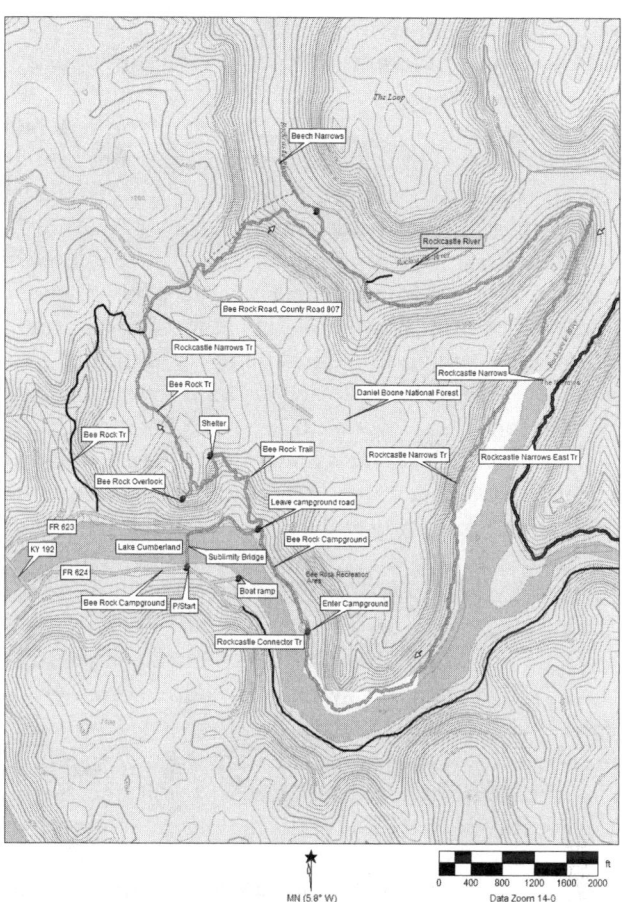

Consider combining adventures such as boating, paddling, camping and fishing, further enjoying Bee Rock Recreation Area when coming here for a hike. And this is a rewarding hike. Start your trek on the south section of Bee Rock Campground, separated by the dammed portion of the Rockcastle River as Lake Cumberland (The north part of Bee Rock Campground is open during the warm season, while the south section of the campground—where this hike starts—is open year-round). Walk across historic Sublimity Bridge, built in the 1930s by the Civilian Conservation Corps, now for hikers only, supplanted by the current Kentucky 192 bridge. Look up at Bee Rock, where you will be in a few minutes. After crossing Sublimity Bridge turn right onto the campground road on the north side of the river, Forest Road 623. Pass a few campsites then look left for the Bee Rock Trail, FT #529, at .3 mile.

Ascend a singletrack path, turning into a bouldery hollow. Work along a ragged cliffline. Curve under a very deep rock shelter fronted with fallen boulders, creating a rockfall arch, at .6 mile. Continue along the base of Bee Rock, rising to find a fissure in the cliffline. Ascend the break and you are atop Bee Rock. Reach a trail intersection at .8 mile. You can go right or left. Head left out to Bee Rock Overlook, descending onto a naked rock slab. Here, look down the dammed Rockcastle River, the KY 192 Bridge, and Sublimity Bridge. Backtrack and continue the Bee Rock Trail amid pine, holly and mountain laurel, leaving the river.

Reach another intersection at 1.2 miles. Here, split right, joining the Rockcastle Narrows Trail (The left turn, the continuation of the Bee Rock Trail, curves back down to Forest Road 623). Cruise flatwoods to reach and cross Bee Rock Road, County Road 807. The Rockcastle Narrows Trail descends by switchbacks. Be careful here, the path is faint in places as you wind a rocky, richly forested slope, filled with wildflowers in spring. The shoals of the Rockcastle River waft up to your ears. Reach the river bottom at 1.8 miles, near the Beech Narrows, rapids on the Rockcastle created by a partly submerged boulder garden. At 1.9 miles, a signed spur trail leads ¼ mile upriver to the Beech Narrows.

The main Rockcastle Narrows Trail continues downriver amid moss, ferns and tulip trees, as well as evergreens. Cross a perennial stream at 2.6 miles, as a user created spur heads down to a campsite. After climbing, the trail levels off. The walking is easy yet beware old logging roads splitting from the signed trail. At 3.3 miles, the trail curves sharply southwest at a significant river bend. Walk between scads of vehicle barrier rocks, as the Rockcastle roars below.

By 3.7 miles, you are well above The Narrows, where the river constricts among huge boulders in the river. When Lake Cumberland is high, The Narrows can be submerged. Other times of the year, such as autumn, the river runs all the way to Bee Rock Campground. The path continues following the bed of the river, allowing good looks at the channel below. By 4.5 miles, you are making another curve. Now-stilled boulders lie along the banks of the land and in the waters below.

At 5.0 miles, the trail emerges at the end of Forest Road 623, and the north side of Bee Rock Campground near campsite #14. From here, follow Forest Road 623 through the campground to Sublimity Bridge. While crossing the river look back up at Bee Rock, and see if you can spot the overlook where you were earlier.

Mileages
- 0.0   Forest Road 624 trailhead at Sublimity Bridge
- 0.3   Join Bee Rock Trail
- 0.6   Rock shelter
- 0.8   Bee Rock Overlook
- 1.2   Right on Rockcastle Narrows Trail
- 1.4   Cross County Road 807
- 1.9   Spur left to Beech Narrows
- 3.3   Trail curves southwest at sharp bend
- 3.7   Rockcastle Narrows below
- 5.0   Return to campground and FR 623
- 5.6   Reach trailhead after crossing Sublimity Bridge

FALLS OF POUNDER BRANCH AND VANHOOK FALLS

Hike Summary: This hike features several waterfalls along its length, culminating in a visit to Vanhook Falls, an especially scenic spiller. Leave the uplands then make your way into the Pounder Branch valley. In this gorgeous hollow you will find a variety of waterfalls along both tributaries of Pounder Branch and Pounder Branch itself while criss crossing these streams. Come to Cane Creek with its rock slabs perfect for sunning, then make a short climb to Vanhook Falls, a classic Kentucky cataract, forming a white curtain dropping 35-feet into a sandstone amphitheater.

DISTANCE: 5.2-miles there-and-back
HIKING TIME: 2.5 hours
DIFFICULTY: Moderate
HIGHLIGHTS: Waterfalls along Pounder Branch, Cane Creek, Vanhook Falls
CAUTIONS: Stream crossings
FEES/PERMITS: No fees or permits required
OTHER TRAIL USERS: None
TRAIL CONTACTS: Daniel Boone National Forest, London Ranger District, 761 South Laurel Road London, KY 40744, (606) 864-4163, www.fs.usda.gov/dbnf

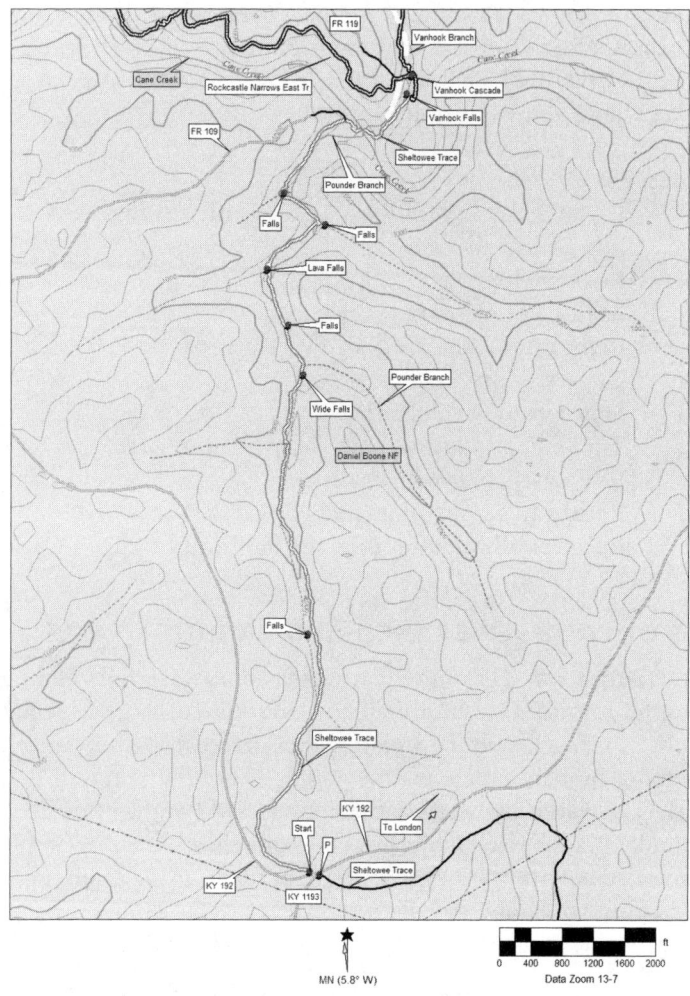

Finding the trailhead: From exit 38 on I-75 near London, head west on KY 192 for 12.2 miles to the intersection with KY 1193 and a trailhead parking area. Follow the Sheltowee Trace leaving north from KY 192. GPS Trailhead Coordinates: N36° 59.865′, W84° 17.093′

Save this hike for a wetter time of year—late fall through spring—and you will be rewarded with a cornucopia of cascades along the streams by which the Sheltowee Trace passes. Furthermore, allow plenty of time for exploring and photographing the waterfalls found along this route,

and still more time for hanging out on Cane Creek, a jewel in the crown of the Daniel Boone National Forest. Even better, consider an overnight camping trip among the streamside flats.

The hike uses Kentucky's longest trail, the Sheltowee Trace. Here the ST enters the primitive and wild Cane Creek Wildlife Management Area, descending to beautiful Cane Creek with its large rock slabs perfect for picnicking or listening to the water flow. It then climbs north past Cane Creek to reach Vanhook Falls, which descend into a sandstone cathedral. Along the way are rockhouses, waterfalls and sandstone bluffs, a truly beautiful parcel of the Bluegrass State.

The Sheltowee Trace leaves north from KY 192 and descends into Pounder Branch valley on a singletrack footpath in upland hardwoods with scattered pines. At .1 mile, veer right and pick up an old roadbed bordered by beech. Enter the upper reaches of the Cane Creek watershed, now on a tributary of Pounder Branch. Here, hemlock, ferns and other moisture favoring vegetation take over. At .4 mile, step over a side stream crossing the trail. At .7 mile, stone steps aid in crossing the tributary you have been following. You are now on the right hand bank of the main tributary, which gathers momentum from flat-bottomed tributaries of its own.

At .8 mile, come to your first falls. This 6-footer makes a short drop over a narrow undercut lip then makes an angled slide over rock into a pool. The Sheltowee Trace crosses the creek by steps again at 1.0 mile—the old roadbed has been left behind. You are traversing inviting flats. The deeper you go in the valley the more beautiful it becomes. By 1.2 miles, you have made two more creek crossings, aided by placed stone steps.

At 1.4 miles, a spur path leads right to a wide and short waterfall with an accompanying big pool. The cascade drops over a stone rim and gathers in a pool far outsizing the size of the stream. The stream soon joins Pounder Branch. The upcoming trail segment is especially scenic. Rock walls rise as Pounder Branch cuts deeper toward Cane Creek. At 1.5 miles, you will hear another waterfall to your right. Here, Pounder Branch tumbles over layers of rock strata, stair-stepping about 10 feet in white grandeur. At 1.7 miles, a side stream crosses the Trace and then tumbles into the Pounder Branch Gorge. This cataract, known as Lava Falls, is difficult but possible to access. After making your way to the bottom of the gorge you will see Lava Falls descend about 25 feet in short vertical drops only to bounce off layer after layer of rock. Additionally, Pounder Branch makes a fall of its own at the point where the Lava Falls ends. Wow!

More aquatic thrills await. At 1.9 miles, as the Sheltowee Trace curves left, look for a side trail leading to the gorge rim. Here, hikers can look on the far side of Pounder Branch for a side stream falling steeply 50 or more feet off the far rim of the gorge. Continue cruising the rim of the gorge on the west side and at 2.2 miles step over another tributary that dives from the rim just a few feet from the trail but unseen. However, the gorge rim is too steep to access unless you walk directly along Pounder Branch to reach the base of this spiller.

At 2.3 miles, a spur path leads left up toward gated Forest Road 109. The Sheltowee Trace bears right, traversing open rock slabs. Look for views of sheer bluffs along Cane Creek below before descending by switchbacks to reach a bridge over Pounder Branch. Note the very difficult to access slide cascade flowing under the Pounder Branch bridge. Span Pounder Branch then come to Cane Creek at 2.4 miles. The clear stream pours over wide rock slabs, which are great for taking a break or sunning or just plain lingering. A wood and metal bridge spans Cane Creek, which is flowing in rapids and slowing in pools. When I recall beautiful places in the Daniel Boone National Forest, this spot comes to mind.

The Sheltowee Trace ascends away from the rugged creek up Vanhook Branch, skirting a series of rock shelters. Burst through rhododendron to reach Vanhook Falls at 2.6 miles. An elevated observation deck with built-in bench makes for an ideal relaxing spot. Here, Vanhook Branch spills 35 feet in a curtain onto a rock base of a circular stone cathedral. The falling water echoes off the rock walls, slowly eroding the scenic valley of Cane Creek into what we see today. If you want to see one more fall, it is but .2 mile farther on the Sheltowee Trace to 10-foot Vanhook Cascade, an angled slide fall.

Mileages
0.0   KY 192 trailhead
0.8   First waterfall
1.7   Lava Falls
2.3   Spur trail to FR 109
2.5   Bridges over Pounder Branch and Cane Creek
2.6   Vanhook Falls
5.2   KY 192 trailhead

LAUREL RIVER LAKE LOOP

Hike Summary: Use the Sheltowee Trace and other nature trails in the greater Holly Bay Recreation Area to fashion a loop that first cruises through upland hardwoods then curves along the shoreline of Laurel River Lake on an easy grade. Enjoy watery views from rocky points and intimate coves as you parallel the shoreline on a well-groomed path. After your walk, consider adding picnicking, swimming, paddling your canoe or kayak at the lake, or even camping at Holly Bay, one of the finest campgrounds in the Daniel Boone National Forest.

DISTANCE: 3.0-mile loop
HIKING TIME: 1.4 hours
DIFFICULTY: Easy
HIGHLIGHTS: Lake views, nearby recreation opportunities

CAUTIONS: None
FEES/PERMITS: No fees or permits required
OTHER TRAIL USERS: Mountain bikers
TRAIL CONTACTS: Daniel Boone National Forest, London Ranger District, 761 South Laurel Road London, KY 40744, (606) 864-4163, www.fs.usda.gov/dbnf

Finding the trailhead: From exit 38 on I-75 near London, head west on KY 192 for 14.2 miles to KY 1193. Turn left on 1193 and follow it for 2.9 miles, passing by Holly Bay campground, to turn left onto Forest Road 611-B and reach the trailhead, a paved parking area. GPS Trailhead Coordinates: N36° 58.157′, W84° 15.992′

This makes an excellent family day hike or a walking adventure for more casual hikers, such as your cousin that likes the idea of hiking but not the sweating and exercise part of hiking. To start the hike from the parking area, walk back toward KY 1193 and turn right, joining the Holly Bay Trail, heading northbound on a singletrack path in hardwoods

Laurel River Lake Loop | 95

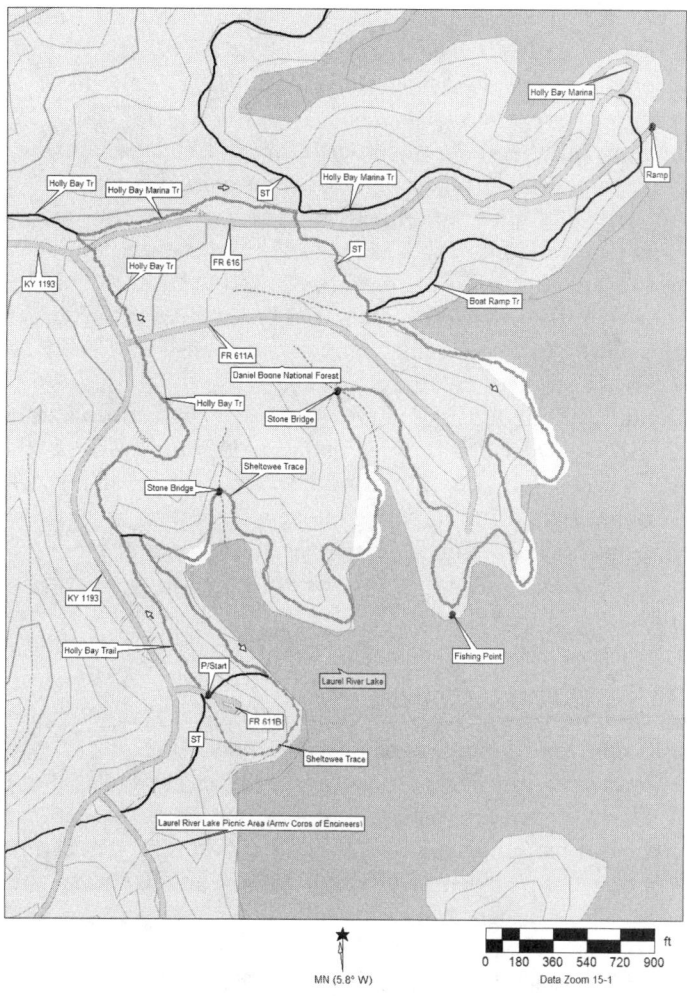

of oak and hickory. At .2 mile, a spur trail leads right to the Sheltowee Trace. Keep straight, working around a dry hollow. Cross Forest Road 611A at .5 mile. The Holly Bay Trail continues north then crosses Forest Road 616, the road to Holly Bay Marina, at .6 mile. Just beyond here, turn right onto the Holly Bay Marina Trail, now heading east and going more down than up on a pleasant wooded pathway. At .9 mile, come to yet another trail intersection. Here, turn right, joining Kentucky's master path, the Sheltowee Trace, southbound. Begin curving into a hollow. At 1.0 mile, the Boat Ramp Trail splits left, but stay straight with the

Sheltowee Trace. These interconnected nature trails are well used by recreationalists at Holly Bay.

Suddenly you are alongside scenic Laurel River Lake, first cruising next to a quiet cove. Black gum, red bud, dogwood and shortleaf pines are found in large numbers near the often-level trail. You will also see plenty of holly trees for which this recreation area is named. Rocky points avail views into the impoundment. In fall and winter, when the lake is drawn down, you can walk onto exposed rocky shores for even more wide-open looks at the lake. Continue the pattern of circling around coves and onto points. At 1.7 miles, a spur trail connects Fishing Point to your left with Forest Road 611A to your right, where anglers park then walk down to the lake to vie for bass, bream and catfish.

Beyond Fishing Point, the Sheltowee Trace curves into a deep cove. Note the stone bridge at 2.0 miles spanning the intermittent stream of the cove. You are well back from the lake. Ahead, pass a small rockhouse on your right. Rock formations are less seen here than other parts of the Daniel Boone National Forest. Step over another small stone bridge in a hollow at 2.6 miles. At 2.7 miles, reach the spur connecting back to the Holly Bay Trail. Keep with the Sheltowee Trace, enjoying more lake panoramas. Head back out to the main lake, then circle below the point of FR 611B. Watch as a paved spur trail splits right up to the trailhead but you can also stay with the Sheltowee Trace as it takes you back to the trailhead from the south side of Forest Road 611B.

I recommend hiking this hike then camping at Holly Bay Campground. That way you can indulge in other activities in this action packed locale. The campground here—with sites for RVers and tent campers—is on one of Kentucky's cleanest, clearest lakes. Holly Bay has eight campsite loops. The campground as a whole is neat, clean, and well kept, making the campsites appealing. There are even walk-in tent sites. Hot showers and water spigots are all about the camp.

Being lakeside makes water recreation at Holly Bay a natural. A boat launch offers easy access from the campground. If you did not bring your own boat, you can rent one at Holly Bay Marina, just a short drive from the campground (You could even walk there on the nature trails). On a hot summer day, you might need the cool waters of the popular swimming area by Laurel River Lake Dam, just south of Holly Bay and run by the Army Corps of Engineers. Also in their domain is a fishing pier for campers without boats. During the summer, naturalist programs are held at the campground amphitheater. The campground can fill on nice weekends, therefore reservations are recommended.

Mileages

0.0	Forest Road 611B trailhead
0.4	Forest Road 611A
0.6	Forest Road 616, right on Holly Bay Marina Trail
0.9	Right on Sheltowee Trace
1.0	Pass Boat Ramp Trail
1.7	Fishing Point
3.0	Forest Road 611B trailhead

FLATWOODS TRAIL

Hike Summary: This hike explores the shores of regal Laurel River Lake, gaining many an aquatic vista as it makes a loop. Starting at the Flatwoods Picnic Area, the easy Flatwoods Trail—despite the name—does offer a little undulation as it circles around the picnic place to end at the Flatwoods Boat Ramp, where a short walk closes the circuit. Most of the time the trail skirts the shore, though in places the path does turn into deep coves. The last part of the circuit uses a forest road to close the loop.

DISTANCE: 2.9-mile loop
HIKING TIME: 1.4 hours
DIFFICULTY: Easy
HIGHLIGHTS: Lake views
CAUTIONS: None
FEES/PERMITS: No fees or permits required
OTHER TRAIL USERS: None
TRAIL CONTACTS: Daniel Boone National Forest, London Ranger District, 761 South Laurel Road London, KY 40744, (606) 864-4163, www.fs.usda.gov/dbnf

Finding the trailhead: From exit 29 on I-75 near Corbin, head west on KY 1783/KY 770 which turns to KY 312 (all on the same road that changes numbers) to turn left on Level Green Road 1.6 miles from the interstate exit. Follow Level Green Road for 2.3 miles then turn left on Flatwoods Road and follow it for 2.2 miles, then veer right into the signed turn for Flatwood Picnic Area. The parking area for the hike is .1 mile beyond the turn into the picnic area. GPS Trailhead Coordinates: N36° 57.479′, W84° 12.528′

Even though the area is known as Flatwoods, there are still a few hills on this hike, very few, as the differential between high and low points on

this hike is less than 150 feet. The name Flatwoods conjures up images of a perfectly level forest, which it is not. This Daniel Boone National Forest recreation area on the shore of Laurel River features not only the Flatwoods Trail winding along Laurel River Lake, but it also has a fine picnic area with widespread shaded picnic tables atop a hill and a sometimes busy boat ramp.

Speaking of the boat ramp, make sure and start this hike at the picnic area trailhead, where no parking fee is charged. If you park at the boat ramp you have to purchase a parking pass. This parking pass is primarily aimed at boaters who park their auto and trailer at the ramp as opposed to us hikers and picnickers up at the picnic area. Definitely bring food with which to dine here at the picnic area. If you are inclined, you could also bring a pole, as bank fishing is very popular here during the warm season.

Like all impoundments in Kentucky, Laurel River Lake is drawn down from fall through winter, to allow water storage space for potential floods. At that time the uppermost part of the lake bottom is exposed. Here, you will see a rocky bottom. Though it may not be as pretty, fall and winter are good times to make this hike, as the motorboat traffic is down, thus making the hike a quiet one.

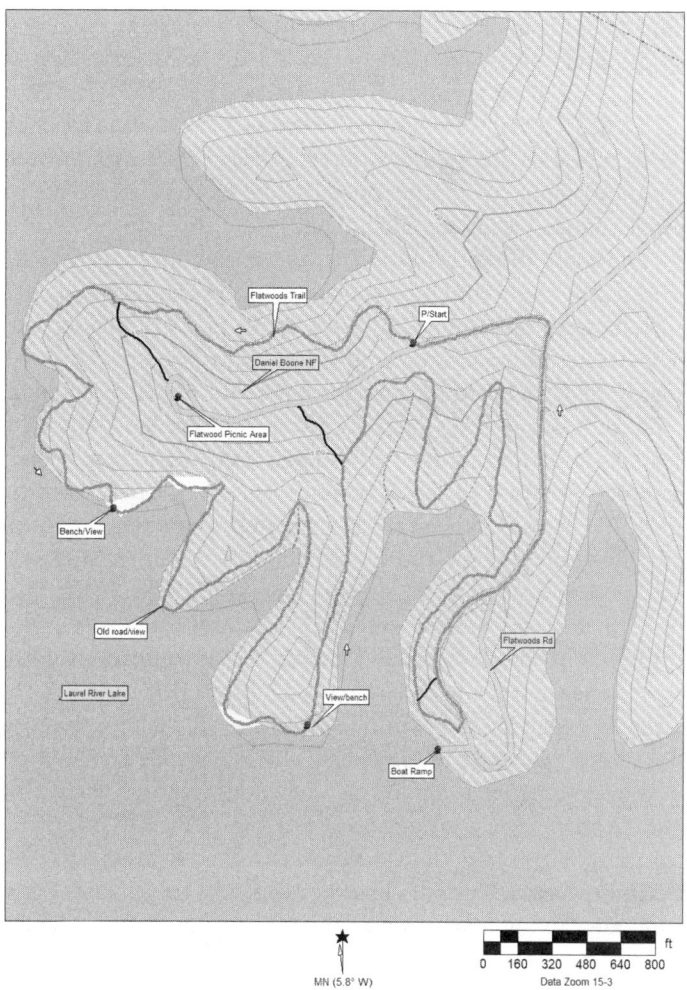

Leave the parking area and join the singletrack Flatwoods Trail, Descend a winding pathway heading west. The trail here was once asphalted but only remnants of the black surface remain. Level off and head west in hardwoods of oaks and beech, with a cove of Laurel River Lake to your right. Hemlocks find their place on this north facing side of the hill. Begin turning in and out of little hollows, now on purely natural surface trail. Contemplation benches offer a place to sit and soak in the woods.

At .3 mile, a spur trail goes left back up to Flatwoods Picnic Area. Stay right here, and begin curving around to the main body of Laurel River

Lake. Short spur trails lead to the shoreline. The vegetation has changed to predominately pines and oaks on the south facing lake edge.

At .7 mile reach a contemplation bench and view into the main channel of the lake. Grove Campground, also part of the Daniel Boone National Forest, stands across the water. Circle around a small watery cove then at 1.0-mile come to another open lake view. Here, an old road crosses the trail. The road was likely abandoned when the dam was erected and Laurel River Lake filled in 1977. The impoundment features 206 miles of shoreline, much of which is managed by the Daniel Boone National Forest, along with the Army Corps of Engineers. The open terrain of the former road does allow for rewarding aquatic panoramas.

Immediately circle around another cove, this one full of standing tree snags. These snags make good fish attractors. On land, the peninsula provides favorable habitat for deer. I have seen them here myself. Pass another contemplation bench with a fine vista to the south at 1.4 miles. From here, the Flatwoods Trail turns away from the water, circling around a narrow lake embayment and makes an incline before reaching a trail intersection at 1.6 miles. Here, a spur leads to the picnic area. Stay right and circle around this narrow lake embayment.

At this point, the trail passes below a few low clifflines with small rockhouses then curves back to one last hollow with a streamlet over which a rock bridge has been built. Make one last dash for the shoreline, soaking in more watery views. Ahead, the Flatwoods boat ramp comes into view and steps lead left to the Flatwoods boat ramp parking area. Then, at 2.4 miles the trail pops out onto the lower parking area near the boat ramp. From here, join paved Flatwoods Road left, northbound, gently climbing away from the boat ramp. At 2.8 miles, turn left toward the picnic area and you are soon at the trailhead, finishing the circuit.

Mileages

0.0	Flatwoods Picnic Area trailhead
0.3	Spur trail leads left to the picnic area
1.6	Spur trail leads left to the picnic area
2.4	Left on Flatwoods Road
2.8	Left on road into Flatwoods Picnic Area
3.0	Flatwoods Picnic Area trailhead

THE SCUTTLE HOLE

Hike Summary: This fun and engaging hike takes you past both geological and aquatic wonders on the heights above Lake Cumberland. Leave the trailhead and quickly come alongside Dutch

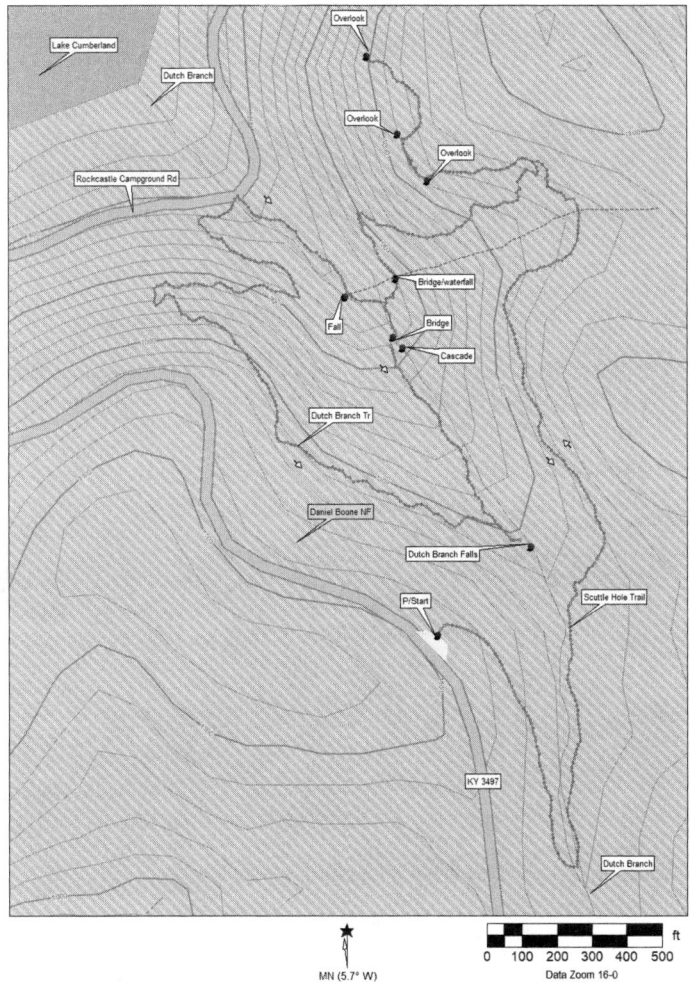

Branch, flowing along a grooved cliffline before dropping 60 feet into a stone cathedral. However, before you visit the base of Dutch Branch Falls, the hike takes a spur to three fantastic overlooks of Lake Cumberland. Next, head to the base of Dutch Branch Falls, viewing other cascades en route, then descend to Rockcastle Campground before climbing back to the trailhead.

DISTANCE: 2.7-mile balloon loop
HIKING TIME: 1.5 hours
DIFFICULTY: Moderate

HIGHLIGHTS: Multiple overlooks, Scuttle Hole, Dutch Branch Falls
CAUTIONS: None
FEES/PERMITS: No fees or permits required
OTHER TRAIL USERS: None
TRAIL CONTACTS: Daniel Boone National Forest, London Ranger District, 761 South Laurel Road London, KY 40744, (606) 864-4163, www.fs.usda.gov/dbnf

Finding the trailhead: From Exit 38 on I-75 near London, head west on KY 192 14 miles to KY 1193. Turn left on KY 1193, and follow it 1 mile to KY 3497. Turn right on KY 3497, and follow it 5.1 miles to the Scuttle Hole trailhead on your right. GPS Trailhead Coordinates: N37° 1.984′, W84° 13.364′

Don't overlook this action-packed hike. There is something to see or appreciate nearly every step of the way, from the unusual flow of Dutch Branch along a low waterworn cliffline, to the three developed overlooks of Lake Cumberland where the Rockcastle River arm of the lake meets the backed up part of the Cumberland River, to the falls along Dutch Branch to still other magnificent clifflines and steep, wildflower rich terrain of the Dutch Branch vale. Furthermore, the hike briefly stops by Rockcastle Campground, a favored auto camping site in the Daniel Boone National Forest. Consider adding an overnight experience at Rockcastle Campground to your Scuttle Hole experience.

The hike innocuously leaves the KY 3497 trailhead on a narrow path, the Scuttle Hole Trail. Curve south into evergreen-heavy Dutch Branch hollow. Quickly cross the upper part of the stream—it may be dry here at times. Turn down Dutch Branch. A low cliffline develops to your left. Dutch Branch flows directly against the cliffline over smooth rock. Enter an area where rock walls form on both sides of the trail and Dutch Branch flows over angled rock, creating a gentle cascade.

At .3 mile, come to the top of a cliffline. Here, Dutch Branch dives 60 feet from the overhung ledge into a semi-circular stone amphitheater. Don't lean over too close, for you will reach the base of the Dutch Branch Falls later. For now, continue cruising along the rim of the gorge, gaining partial views in brushy vegetation. Dutch Branch valley widens below.

Step over an intermittent streambed then reach a trail intersection at .6 mile. Here, stay right toward the overlooks before returning here to cut through the Scuttle Hole. Climb a bit then come to the first overlook, bordered by fence. This one offers a southward view up Dutch Branch and a westerly vantage down to Lake Cumberland. Pines and other evergreens frame the landscape. Continue to quickly reach the second overlook, located on an outcrop with land falling away below. These overlooks needed no clearing—they are natural vista spots. However, the fencing helps hikers feel at ease, especially those with kids in tow. The final overlook is reached at .8 mile. Here, you can gaze down the Rockcastle River arm of Lake Cumberland as well as across at the cliffs above and the embayment of Pole Bridge Branch. In aggregate, these three vistas will hold their own against any overlook in the Daniel Boone National Forest.

Backtrack from the overlooks then turn down into the Scuttle Hole. Inset steps lead you down a narrow crevice in the cliffline. This is Kentucky hiking at its finest. Pass an impressive rockhouse and keep descending to bridge a streamlet just above a 10-foot waterfall that is difficult to see from the trail. At 1.1 miles, meet the Dutch Branch Trail. Head left here up the defile of Dutch Branch, quickly bridging Dutch Branch near a small cascade. Ahead, tackle the steepest part of the hike, working your way up the side of Dutch Branch among gigantic mossy boulders.

At 1.2 miles, a spur goes left to the base of Dutch Branch Falls. Follow the spur to reach a massive semicircular rockhouse. Here, you can see Dutch Branch issue from the stone lip to splatter onto a rock jumble below. The cataract can nearly dry up in late summer and fall but is a sight in the springtime and also when frozen in the grip of winter.

From here, backtrack and continue the Dutch Branch Trail. Cruise alongside a magnificent cliffline. In winter, when the leaves are off the trees, you can look across Dutch Branch to see the developed overlooks. At 1.6 miles, the trail drops away from the cliffline, descending a steep slope via switchbacks. Reach the road of Rockcastle Campground at 1.8 miles. Walk just a few feet on the road to bridge Dutch Branch and pick up the balance of the Dutch Branch Trail. Ascend the steep valley, passing a 6-foot waterfall at the confluence of Dutch Branch and a tributary.

At 1.9 miles, complete the loop of Dutch Branch. From here, you climb back through the Scuttle Hole, counting the steps while rising, then backtrack to the trailhead, completing the exciting hike at 2.7 miles.

Mileages

0.0	Scuttle Hole trailhead
0.3	Top of Dutch Branch Falls
0.6	Right to three overlooks, backtrack
1.1	Left on Dutch Branch Trail
1.8	Rockcastle Campground road
1.9	Begin backtrack on Scuttle Hole Trail
2.7	Scuttle Hole trailhead

LAKESIDE SOUTH LOOP

Hike Summary: This rewarding circuit hike offers a variety of scenery, including lakeside woods with watery views, intimate stream valleys, cascades, rock outcrops and backpacking possibilities, all of which start at a shady auto accessible campground. Your clockwise loop leaves Rockcastle Campground then cruises up Ned Branch to a ridgetop. From there, descend along shoals of Twin Branch to reach Lake Cumberland, where you wander above the shoreline for miles, crossing small streams and cruising woodlands before returning to the trailhead.

DISTANCE: 8.5-mile loop
HIKING TIME: 4.5 hours

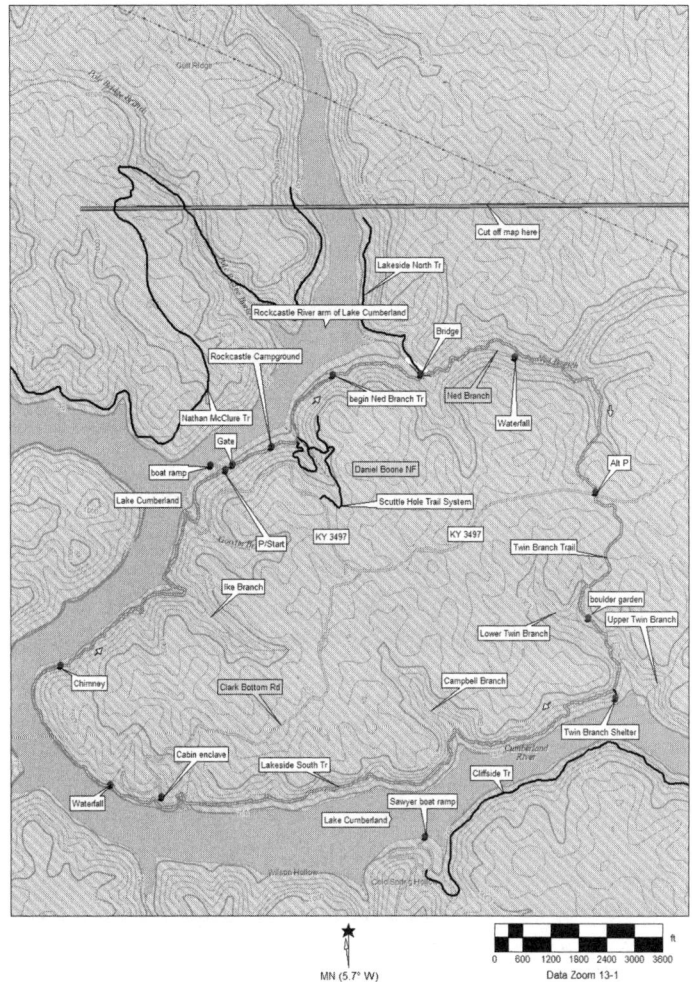

DIFFICULTY: Moderate-difficult
HIGHLIGHTS: Lake views, springtime cascades, trail shelter
CAUTIONS: None
FEES/PERMITS: No fees or permits required
OTHER TRAIL USERS: None
TRAIL CONTACTS: Daniel Boone National Forest, London Ranger District, 761 South Laurel Road London, KY 40744, (606) 864-4163, www.fs.usda.gov/dbnf

Finding the trailhead: From Exit 38 on I-75 near London, head west on KY 192 14 miles to KY 1193. Turn left on KY 1193, and

follow it 1 mile to KY 3497. Turn right on KY 3497, and follow it 6 miles to reach the large boat ramp parking area just before entering the campground. Do not park in the campground. GPS Trailhead Coordinates: N36° 57.643', W84° 21.164'

This is one of the DBNF's better circuit hikes, and presents a variety of sights and scenery along the way. It takes place at the confluence of the now-dammed Cumberland River and Rockcastle River, the current locale of ribbon-like Lake Cumberland, from which steep, richly wooded hillsides rise to rock-capped ridges. Consider overnighting at Rockcastle Campground, open year-round, where the trek begins. However, winter is also a good time to make this hike, as the lake boat traffic will be nearly nil, making for a quiet experience. Spring will offer showy wildflowers. A trail shelter adds backpacking possibilities. Lake Cumberland opens the prospect of fishing, swimming, boating or paddling.

Head north from the boat ramp parking area to enter deeply shaded Rockcastle Campground, following the campground access road. Campsites and restrooms stand near the road. Beech trees rise regal overhead. Campsites spur from the paved campground road. At .3 mile, pass a pair of paths leading right, part of the Scuttle Hole nature trail system. Continue through the campground to reach a road turnaround at .6 mile. Here, leave the campground road join the Ned Branch Trail, a singletrack footpath amid lush forest. Curve into the Ned Branch valley on a slope.

At 1.1 miles, reach a hiker bridge spanning Ned Branch, amid big boulders. Here, the Lakeside North Trail splits left to dead end after .7 mile. Our hike heads right from the hiker bridge, up Ned Branch, a cornucopia of Kentucky beauty—massive sandstone boulders, clifflines, tall trees, and a clear stream. At 1.6 miles, pass a seasonal 8-foot waterfall dripping from a cliffline above. At 1.8 miles, bridge the stream again, then turn south, ascending a tributary of Ned Branch. The trail criss-crosses the tributary amid boulders, rockhouses and evergreens, climbing all the while.

Emerge onto then cross KY 3497 at 2.6 miles. Join the Twin Branch Trail. By 2.9 miles, you are dropping into a tributary of Lower Twin Branch. Rockhouses form on both sides of the steep vale. Descend along the stream as it cascades in sheets, eventually falling well below the path. At 3.3 miles, the trail weaves through a boulder garden, beautiful routing. Cross Lower Twin Branch then start curving west to parallel the shore of Lake Cumberland. A spur drops left to the Twin Branch trail shelter at 3.7 miles. This three-sided Adirondack-style hut with an open front faces Lake Cumberland.

From here, the Twin Branch Trail arbitrarily becomes the Lakeside South Trail. At 3.9 miles, a pair of switchbacks brings you closer to the shoreline but still well above the summer pool level. Cruise the sloped woods westerly. Cross Campbell Branch in a hollow at 4.5 miles. From here, the trail continues westerly, traversing boulder jumbles and turning into hollows with intermittent streams, some spanned with small stone bridges, made onsite with rock slabs.

At 5.9 miles, reach a stream, gravel road and the beginning of a summer home enclave. Keep west across the road. The Lakeside South Trail continues curving westerly above the shoreline, with the homes and their access road above the trail. By 6.3 miles, you have left the homes behind and turn into a hollow, where an unnamed stream drops over a cliff about 12 feet, creating a waterfall below the trail. This cataract can nearly dry up by autumn.

Slowly but surely you are following the dammed Cumberland River as it makes a big bend to the north. The going is easy and the trail is fairly level under an abundant tree canopy. Pass by an old rock chimney of a cabin at 7.1 miles. Curve into the hollow of Ike Branch, bridging the stream at 7.8 miles. Note the large beech trees in this hollow. Make one last run along the lake before turning into the hollow of Goodin Branch.

The Lakeside South Trail ends where it emerges onto KY 3497 at 8.2 miles. From here, head left on KY 3497 and descend to reach the boat ramp parking area and trailhead at 8.5 miles, completing the rewarding loop hike.

Mileages

0.0	Entrance to Rockcastle Campground
0.3	Pass Scuttle Hole trails
0.6	Begin Ned Branch Trail
1.1	Wooden bridge over Ned Branch
2.6	Cross KY 3497
3.3	Boulder garden
3.7	Twin Branch trail shelter
5.9	Summer home enclave road
6.3	Waterfall
7.1	Chimney
8.2	Left on KY 3497
8.5	Boat ramp parking area beside Rockcastle Campground

BEAVER CREEK WILDERNESS LOOP

Hike Summary: This circuit hike takes place in the rugged Beaver Creek Wilderness, characterized by faint trails, little signage and challenging conditions. However, if you are looking for such a place the untamed area will do the trick. This loop wanders along a high ridge before dropping to Beaver Creek. Here, make your way up the stream on a dim track to reach an old wooden road bridge. From this spot, wind your way back to the trailhead.

DISTANCE: 4.1-mile loop
HIKING TIME: 2.5 hours
DIFFICULTY: Difficult due to trail conditions
HIGHLIGHTS: Wild area, Beaver Creek
CAUTIONS: Faint, unmarked trails in wilderness
FEES/PERMITS: No fees or permits required
OTHER TRAIL USERS: None
TRAIL CONTACTS: Daniel Boone National Forest, Stearns Ranger District, 3320 US 27 North, Whitley City, KY 42653, (606)376-5323, www.fs.usda.gov/dbnf

Finding the trailhead: From the Stearns Ranger Station just north of Whitley City, drive north on US 27 for 9.2 miles then turn right

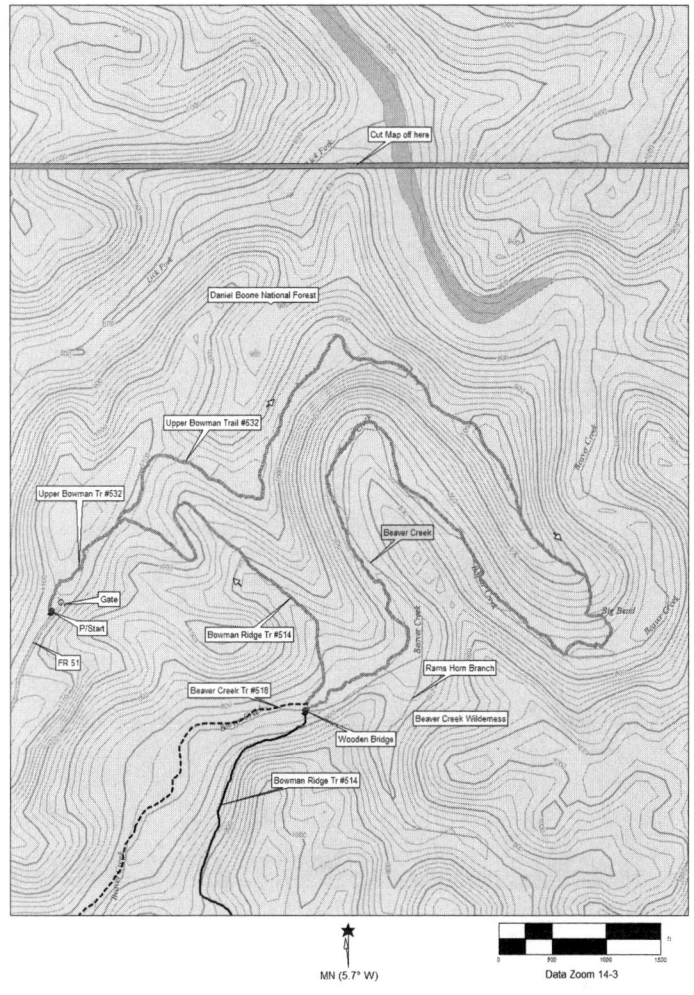

on paved Bower Road and follow it for 2.2 miles to turn right on gravel Forest Road 51. Stay with FR 51 for 2.4 miles to the Upper Bowman trailhead, on your left, the second trailhead you will pass. GPS Trailhead Coordinates: N36° 55.281′, W84° 25.835′

Beaver Creek Wilderness covers nearly 5,000 acres of remote terrain within the Beaver Creek watershed, a tributary of the mighty Cumberland River. Including formerly settled lands, and a coal mining berg of the 1800s, the parcel has reverted to its untamed state since its 1975 federal wilderness designation. In fact, Beaver Creek is so wild now, hikers have to navigate nearly trackless, overgrown woods on faint rough

pathways. If you are an inexperienced hiker here, I recommend using a GPS downloaded with topo maps to keep apprised of your whereabouts. Beware of wilderness maps you may find on the Internet—many of them are inaccurate or suggestive of trails and routes that may be just faded footbeds in reality. Furthermore, long pants and a long sleeve shirt are recommended while hiking here. What faint paths you find are overgrown and can be brushy to the extreme. Briers can be problematic in places. Do not come here in summer—the vegetation will be too thick. I recommend fall through mid-spring. The woods will be more open, the brush will be down and the going easier. Beaver Creek Wilderness is one place where proper preparation will pay bigger than average dividends.

From the trailhead parking area, as you face the signboard, walk behind the signboard to pick up the Upper Bowman Trail #532. Head right to join a grassy track, passing around a pole gate. Ahead, at .1 mile, the signed trail leaves right again as a singletrack path. Roll northeast amid briery woods of maple, oak and dogwood to reach a signed trail intersection at .2 mile. Stay left with the Upper Bowman Trail #532, as your return route Bowman Ridge Trail #514 splits right.

Begin rolling on a high ridge around which Beaver Creek makes a 180 degree turn, with sharp drop-offs on both sides. A sign marks your official entrance into Beaver Creek Wilderness at 1.0 mile. The trail curves southeasterly and descends, rolling over several earthen vehicle/erosion barriers. Come to Beaver Creek at 1.7 miles. Here, at a place known as Big Bend, what has been of the path you have been following degenerates. At this point expect to work your way up the valley, upstream, keeping on the right bank of scenic Beaver Creek, clambering over blowdowns, squeezing past steep spots below bluffs and cruising thickly vegetated flats. Look for sawn logs and a faint footbed to help keep you on the right track.

Despite the challenges, the beauty is undeniable. The clear waterway gurgles over a rocky bed beside rock, gravel and sand bars. Small picturesque islands rise from the stream. Cliffs stand near and far. A riot of vegetation thickens the vale. At 2.0 miles, a bluff rises on the right. The route squeezes between Beaver Creek to the left and the low bluff to the right. Flats open on the far side of the stream, alternating in pools and shoals.

At 2.4 miles, Beaver Creek makes a sharp left curve, nearly 180 degrees. A sandbar forms on the inside bend. The route curves with the stream. After making it through this slender segment, flats again open on the right hand side of the creek. At 3.0 miles, step over a seasonal stream flowing into Beaver Creek. You can make it to the wooden former road bridge spanning Beaver Creek at 3.1 miles without crossing Beaver Creek, making this hike a wintertime possibility. The bridge makes a good place to relax. And you will know for sure where you are. Look upstream and downstream at free flowing Beaver Creek from the bridge.

A faded route, ambitiously named Beaver Creek Trail #518, continues up Beaver Creek. Our track from here becomes much easier to follow. From the bridge, trace an old forest road with a firm base northeasterly from the wooden bridge. This is the Bowman Ridge Trail #514 (Heading south from the wooden bridge the Bowman Ridge Trail rises to the trailhead on Swain Ridge). Trace the old forest road on a solid bed. The going is much easier than the preceding part of the loop.

Work up a hollow then curve around its head, rising to xeric woods. At 3.7 miles, a sign notes the wilderness boundary. Just ahead, the trail splits right from the old forest road. A final uptick leads you the intersection where you were before. From here, head left, backtracking to the trailhead.

Mileages
0.0   Bowman trailhead on FR 51
0.2   Upper Bowman Trail stays left while Bowman Ridge trail leaves right
1.7   Reach Beaver Creek
3.1   Wooden bridge over Beaver Creek
3.9   Complete loop portion of hike
4.1   Bowman trailhead on FR 51

BARK CAMP CREEK CASCADES AND SHELTER

Hike Summary: Arguably Kentucky's most scenic stream, Bark Camp Creek and the valley through which it flows present a menagerie of small waterfalls, regal clifflines and arresting rockhouses en route to Bark Camp Creek Cascades, a series of singing cataracts gracing the waterway's lower reaches. A side trip to Bark Camp Creek trail shelter allows you to experience a bit of the Cumberland River, into which Bark Camp Creek flows. Once down there, a challenging yet avoidable stream crossing allows you to make a loop up lower Bark Camp Creek.

DISTANCE: 5.8-mile balloon loop
HIKING TIME: 3 hours
DIFFICULTY: Moderate, does have one tough but avoidable creek crossing
HIGHLIGHTS: Bark Camp Creek Cascades, lesser waterfalls, geology
CAUTIONS: Avoidable creek crossing
FEES/PERMITS: No fees or permits required
OTHER TRAIL USERS: None
TRAIL CONTACTS: Daniel Boone National Forest, London Ranger District, 761 South Laurel Road London, KY 40744, (606) 864-4163, www.fs.usda.gov/dbnf

Finding the trailhead: From exit 25 on I-75 near Corbin, take US 25W south for 4.7 miles to turn right onto KY 1193 north. Follow KY 1193 north for 4.6 miles, then continue straight on Bee Creek Road. Follow Bee Creek Road for 1.2 miles, then turn left onto FR 193. Follow FR 193 for 1.8 miles to reach the Bark Camp trailhead on your right at a curve before FR 193 spans Bark Camp Creek by culvert. GPS Trailhead Coordinates: N36° 54.282′, W84° 16.854′

Bark Camp Creek Cascades and Shelter

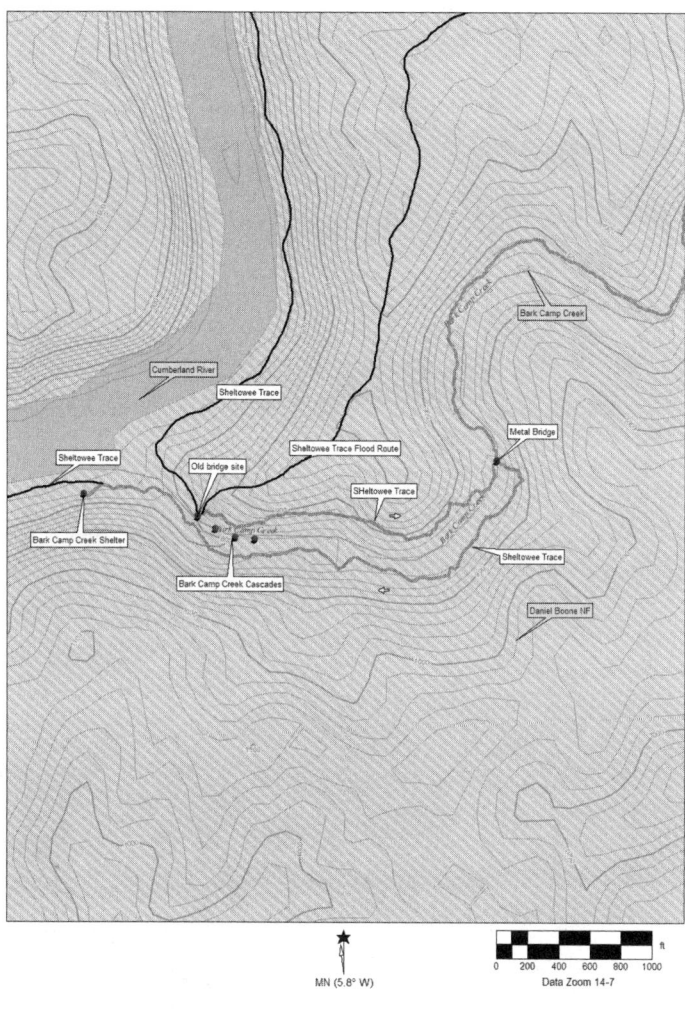

The continual beauty of Bark Camp Creek will catch your eye, even as the scenes change before you, from wooded streamside flats to overhanging clifflines to bluffs lording over a dashing stream. The geological presence enhances the scenery but makes hiking down the creek a challenge at times. The lower portion of the creek presents numerous tiered falls, cataracts and shoals, collectively known as the Bark Camp Creek Cascades. You will have an opportunity to observe and record them after visiting Bark Camp Creek Shelter.

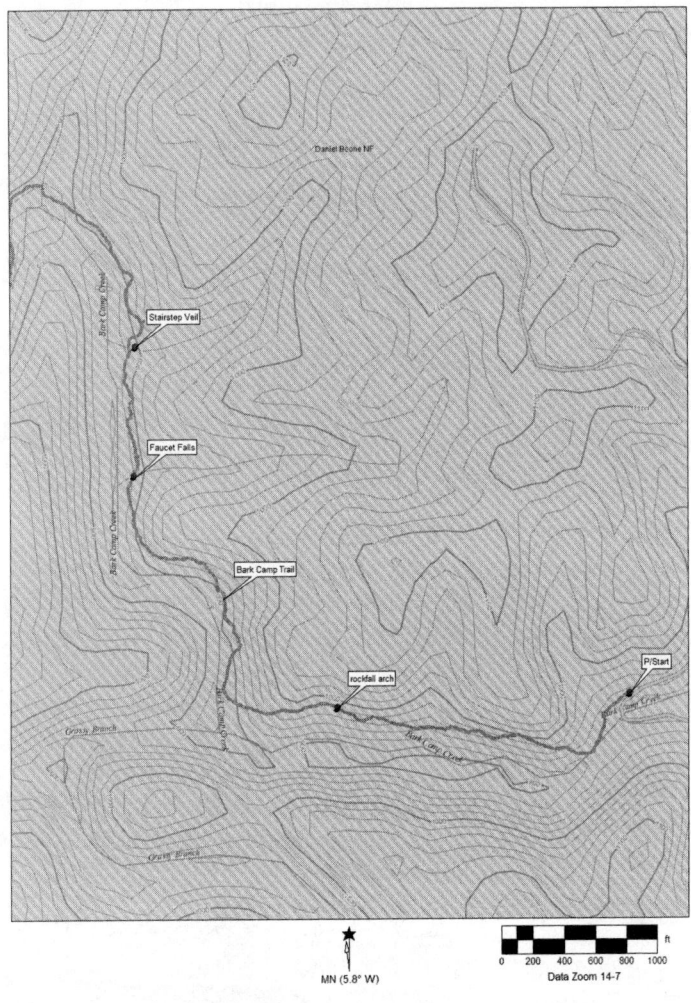

Leave the trailhead heading downstream on the right hand bank of Bark Camp Creek in woodland of evergreens and black birch. Immediately come along your first cliffline. Bark Camp Creek gurgles below. Surprisingly turn right and climb, coming alongside yet another cliffline. Soon drop back along Bark Camp Creek, walking by a deep swimming hole bordered by big boulders. Rhododendron grows in profusion and often crowds the trail. At .4 mile, the Bark Camp Trail passes under a fallen boulder that forms a roof over the path—a rockfall arch.

Ahead, bisect a narrow spot between a cliff and another deep pool. Open onto a bigger flat as the stream curves north and has added the waters of Grassy Branch to its flow. Saddle along more clifflines and at .9 mile saunter under the overhang of an immense boulder, then come to Faucet Falls, a slender spiller that makes a 40-foot ribbon-like drop from a cliffline above you. The low flow stream can nearly dry up in late summer and autumn. Continue along the cliffline to reach the 40-foot Stairstep Veil at 1.1 miles. This is an intriguing low flow waterfall that drops over a series of stair step ledges then makes a sheet dive from an overhanging cliffline, splattering onto broken rocks below.

At 1.3 miles, step over a tributary coming in from a hollow to your right. The stream and trail are curving mightily, trying to cut through the Cumberland Plateau to reach the Cumberland River. Look for small streamside yellow sand beaches and islands in Bark Camp Creek. You've been on the right hand bank the whole way. At 2.2 miles, near a modest slide cascade, reach the Sheltowee Trace and a bridge over Bark Camp Creek. The old bridge was well downstream but this one is better located for long term survival from sporadic floods. It stands atop two boulders on either side of the creek.

Here, cross the long bridge, joining the Sheltowee Trace southbound then continue downriver on the steep south side of the Bark Camp Creek. Wind along the deep hollow. Soon you can hear Bark Camp Creek Cascades well below. At 2.7 miles, near a big rock overhang, the old Sheltowee Trace route once crossed Bark Camp Creek on a bridge of which you can see the foundations. Remember this spot for later.

Now, continue down the Sheltowee Trace, meeting the spur trail leading left to Bark Camp shelter. Take the spur, reaching the shelter at 2.9 miles. The three-sided Adirondack style wood refuge is open on the front. A large rock palisade rises behind the shelter while flat full of wildflowers in spring stand in front. From here, backtrack to the old Sheltowee Trace bridge site. If Bark Camp Creek isn't raging, make the rock hop/boulder climb across the stream. Once across, reach a trail intersection. Here, the Sheltowee Trace curves out to the Cumberland River and heads downstream toward Mouth of Laurel boat ramp, while the other end of the Trace heads up Bark Camp Creek. The Sheltowee Trace Alternate Flood Route climbs a ridgeline then reunites 3 miles later with the Sheltowee Trace.

Head right, up the Trace and up Bark Camp Creek, but not before exploring and photographing the lowermost Bark Camp Creek Cascades, a series of drops divided by pools, complemented with ample slab rocks for viewing. Keep up the north bank of Bark Camp Creek, passing other smaller cascades, including modest water slides. The trail on this side is closer to the creek. Return to the metal bridge over Bark Camp Creek at 3.6 miles. Leave the Sheltowee Trace and make the 2.1 mile backtrack to the trailhead, enjoying more of the geological, aquatic and floral finery of the Bark Camp Creek valley.

Mileages
- 0.0 Bark Camp trailhead
- 0.9 Faucet Falls
- 1.1 Stairstep Veil
- 2.2 Cross metal bridge on the Sheltowee Trace
- 2.7 Old Sheltowee Trace bridge crossing, Bark Camp Creek Cascades
- 2.9 Bark Camp shelter
- 3.1 Cross Bark Camp Creek at old bridge site, Bark Camp Creek Cascades
- 3.6 Reach metal bridge on Sheltowee Trace, backtrack
- 5.8 Bark Camp trailhead

DOG SLAUGHTER FALLS STAR CREEK FALLS AND SHELTER

Hike Summary: This gorgeous hike visits waterways big and small as well as waterfalls big and small. Start by hiking down the scenic Dog Slaughter Creek valley to visit iconic Dog Slaughter Falls, a 20-foot classic spiller deep within geological amazement for which the Daniel Boone National Forest is known. From there turn down the brawling Cumberland River on the Sheltowee Trace amid big trees, bigger boulders and rapids to find delicate, ribbon-like 70-foot Star Creek Falls and the Star Creek backcountry shelter.

DISTANCE: 7.6-mile there-and-back
HIKING TIME: 4 hours
DIFFICULTY: Moderate-difficult due to irregular trail terrain
HIGHLIGHTS: Waterfalls, hiking along Kentucky wild river
CAUTIONS: None
FEES/PERMITS: No fees or permits required
OTHER TRAIL USERS: None
TRAIL CONTACTS: Daniel Boone National Forest, London Ranger District, 761 South Laurel Road London, KY 40744, (606) 864-4163, www.fs.usda.gov/dbnf

Dog Slaughter Falls Star Creek Falls and Shelter | 119

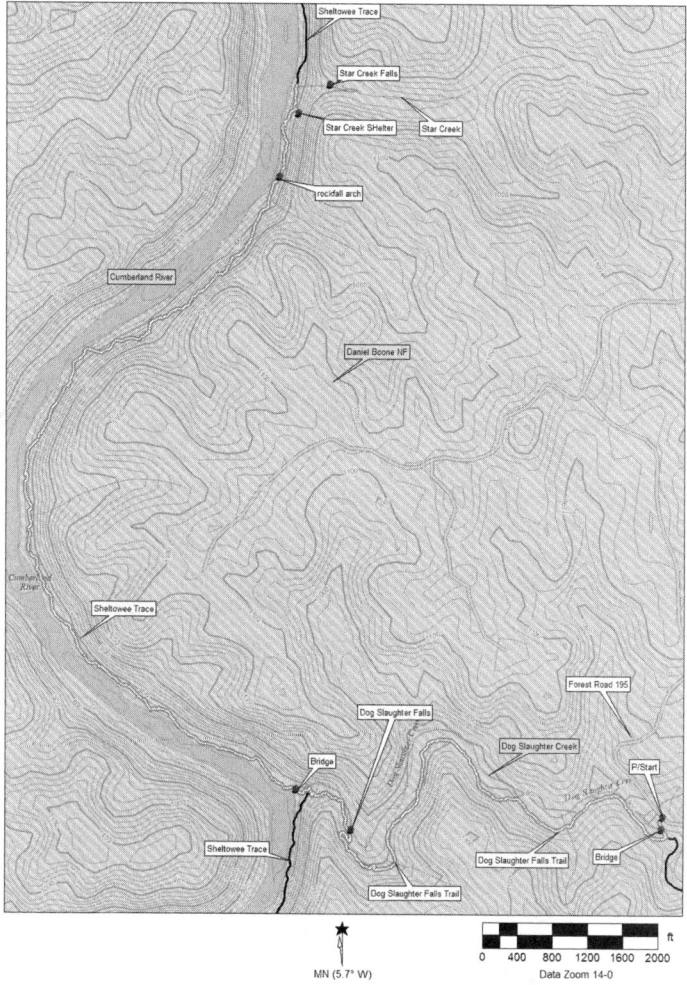

Finding the trailhead: From exit 25 near Corbin, take US 25W south for 7.5 miles to KY 90. Veer right onto KY 90 west for 2.2 miles to reach Forest Road 195 and follow it for 3 miles to the lower Dog Slaughter Creek Trail parking on your left heading downhill as FR 195 curves right. GPS Trailhead Coordinates: N36° 51.562', W84° 17.987'

This hike presents eye-pleasing wild scenery from beginning to end. The terrain is beautiful but rugged. And so are the trails, despite no major

elevation changes. The hike does have short steep segments and sections of working around and among bluffs and clifflines that keep you watching your step. Take your time for safety's sake and to absorb every detail of this locale.

The hike leaves Forest Road 193 on a spur then quickly descends to a flat and wooden trail bridge spanning South Fork Dog Slaughter Creek. Reach Dog Slaughter Falls Trail on the far end of the bridge. Here, turn right, downstream. The singletrack path works its way through a deeply wooded valley mixed with a heavy dose of boulders, clifflines and rockhouses. Just downstream North Fork Dog Slaughter Creek adds its flow to the main stream. Mosses, ferns and evergreens rise in a primeval setting. At .3 mile, the path swings around a feeder branch then cuts beneath a bluff. More clifflines and rock shelters lie ahead as the trail undulates along the creek. Massive boulders lie in repose mid-stream. At .7 mile, the trail passes a big pool bordered with bigger boulders.

Ahead, bisect a hemlock grove threatened by the encroaching hemlock wooly adelgid, a non-native insect killing hemlocks. Step over a tributary of Dog Slaughter Creek at 1.0 mile. The path makes a big bend, following the curves of Dog Slaughter Creek. At 1.2 miles, peer over a rock ledge at the top of Dog Slaughter Falls. Be patient. The trail finds a breach in the bluff and drops steeply to the base of the cataract. Here, at 1.3 miles, you can gain a head-on view of the 20-foot curtain-like straight drop, half circled in a stone grotto and fronted by dark boulders. The scene is one of the finest in the entire Daniel Boone National Forest.

Beyond the falls, continue downstream, fighting through an incredible boulder garden bordered by a stream-echoing cliffline. Meet the Sheltowee Trace at 1.4 miles. Turn right here, dipping to the water then reaching an angled hiker span crossing Dog Slaughter Creek. The backdrop is outstanding, and personifies wild Kentucky. Here, you can peer down a massive boulder jumble through which Dog Slaughter Creek flows to the Cumberland River.

Pick through more stone and then saddle alongside the mighty Cumberland. Shoals are common, coursing through boulders. Oaks, dogwoods and pines become more prevalent along this section of southwest-facing, sometimes-sandy trail. At 2.5 miles, the Sheltowee Trace bridges a small stream. The river is bending right and the shore is no longer southwest facing, thus has more moisture loving vegetation such as beech and rhododendron. Work among rock formations, including a cliffline at 3.1 miles that you follow directly alongside for a quarter mile.

At 3.5 miles, the Sheltowee Trace leads under a rockfall arch, where a pair of boulders lies on top of two adjacent boulders. Move fast—you never know when the agglomeration is going to topple. . . . At 3.7 miles, come to the Star Creek shelter, located on a very short spur trail. This three-sided Adirondack style wood refuge stands to the right of the trail. The front is open and faces toward the Cumberland River. Backpackers hiking all or part of the Sheltowee Trace use it as an overnighting option. A fire ring stands in front of the shelter.

Your final highlight is just ahead, and at 3.8 miles reach Star Creek. You can look up from the trail at the 70-foot ribbon of water pouring over a rock face broken by small ledges then down through the air to splatter into a rock pile below. It takes some effort but you can scramble to the cataract. Though it may not be as voluminous as Dog Slaughter Falls, Star Creek Falls offers aquatic beauty of its own.

Mileages

0.0	Lower Dog Slaughter Falls trailhead
1.3	Dog Slaughter Falls
1.4	Right on Sheltowee Trace
2.5	Bridge small stream
3.1	Long cliffline
3.5	Rockfall arch
3.7	Star Creek shelter
3.8	Star Creek Falls
7.6	Lower Dog Slaughter Falls trailhead

CUMBERLAND FALLS DOG SLAUGHTER FALLS

Hike Summary: Not only do you get to visit two of Kentucky's most scenic waterfalls but also walk along the wild Cumberland River through a gorge of magnificent beauty. Starting at Cumberland Falls State Park, the hike first visits Cumberland Falls, a busy spot with multiple designated overlooks. From there, head along the Cumberland River amidst geological and aquatic wonderment, passing other, lesser-known waterfalls. Enter the Daniel Boone National Forest to find Dog Slaughter Falls in a deep valley framed in wood and stone, making its own worthy drop. Your return trip will yield more beauty in this gorgeous slice of the Bluegrass State.

DISTANCE: 7.0-mile there-and-back
HIKING TIME: 3.8 hours
DIFFICULTY: Moderate-difficult due to irregular terrain in places
HIGHLIGHTS: Cumberland Falls, Cumberland River rapids, waterfalls, Dog Slaughter Falls
CAUTIONS: Short steep sections, irregular terrain
FEES/PERMITS: No fees or permits required
OTHER TRAIL USERS: None
TRAIL CONTACTS: Cumberland Falls State Resort Park, 7351 Highway 90, Corbin, KY 40701, (606) 528-4121, http://parks.ky.gov/parks/resortparks/cumberland-falls/

Finding the trailhead: From Exit 25 on I-75 near Corbin, take US 25W south for 7.5 miles to KY 90. Turn right and take KY 90 west for 8.3 miles, turning right into the large Cumberland Falls parking area before the bridge over the Cumberland River. GPS Trailhead Coordinates: N36° 50.2620′, W84° 20.6157′

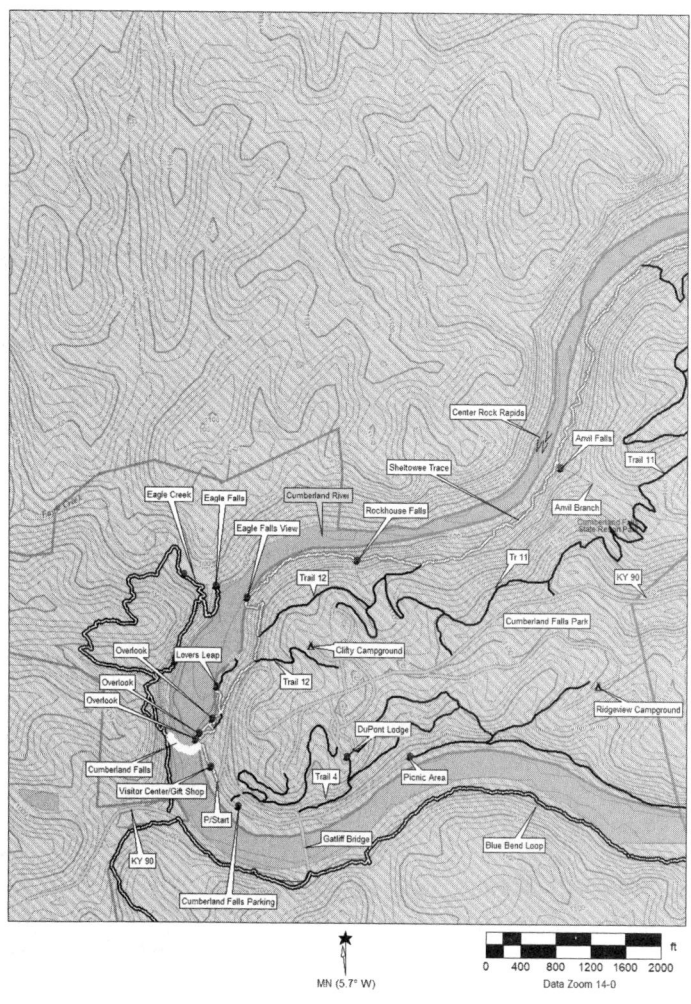

On this hike the Sheltowee Trace, also known as the Moonbow Trail in Cumberland Falls State Park, heads north along the mighty Cumberland River to see Kentucky's most powerful falls roar over a sandstone ledge, then meanders through a boulder garden of designated state wild river beauty in the Cumberland River gorge. The Trace then leaves Cumberland Falls State Park to reenter the Daniel Boone National Forest.

Leave the west end of the Cumberland Falls parking area to pass the gift shop and visitor center. Cumberland Falls is just downstream from the buildings. The entire flow of the Cumberland River forms a 125-foot wide curtain that plummets 67 feet in a roar of power. The mist rising

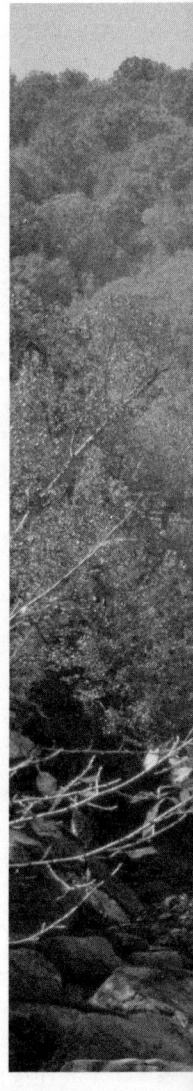

from the water's descent creates a "moonbow," purportedly one of only two moonbows in the world. A full moon shines on the fall's mist and creates the moonbow; much like the sun creates a rainbow during daytime at Cumberland Falls. The state park's website specifies the monthly dates and times of the moonbows (provided the moon is not obscured by clouds) on their website.

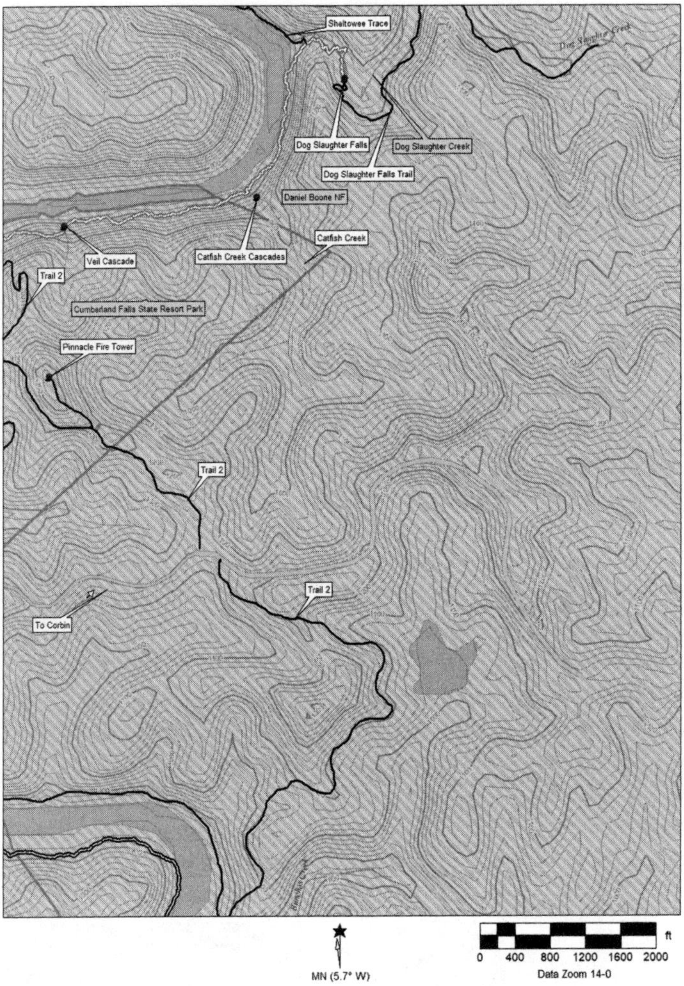

Stay on the trails closest to the river to enjoy multiple overlooks. First, look at the falls from above, then skirt along a bluff to see it from

below. This viewpoint is close enough to be misted on when the falls are up and the wind blowing. A concrete trail takes you downriver to more overlooks, reaching Lovers Leap at .3 mile. This gives you the best view of the falls but can be a crowded place. Note the memorial to Kentucky native T. Coleman DuPont. He purchased the falls and the land around it for the state park. Soak in the misty powerful falls, the huge pool below and bluffs across the waterway, a big scale scene.

Backtrack a bit then pick up the Moonbow Trail/Sheltowee Trace at

.4 mile, and resume downriver. Come close to KY 90, climbing past a pair of intersections with Trail 12. A series of switchbacks and finally a staircase lead you back down along the Cumberland River—a designated Kentucky Wild River—at .7 mile. The crowds have been left behind. Ahead, look across for Eagle Falls.

On the Cumberland River, massive boulders line the watercourse, now much narrower below Cumberland Falls than above. Crashing rapids periodically occur on the river. The going is slow on the rocky tread, while big bluffs tower over hikers. At 1.1 miles, the trail splits right, passing under a low flow slender fall, dropping 20 feet from a rockhouse, Rock House Falls. Follow the Rock House Trail. The old Sheltowee Trace has been abandoned here. Climb beyond into woods, passing a trail leading uphill into the park trail network. The Rock House/Sheltowee Trace descends back toward the river.

Rejoin the old Trace. The rock ramparts briefly recede and the Trace cuts through bottomland. Watch for sand beaches and river birch trees. The gorge soon closes in again and the Trace passes under a massive rock shelter. Evergreen forests rise on the hillsides. At 1.6 miles, Anvil Branch forms a 20-foot, low-flow slide cascade as it pours down a ledge and disappears into a boulder field then flows under the trail. Just ahead, you can walk out onto a boulder to view Center Rock Rapids, where the Cumberland crashes white through a boulder jumble.

The singletrack path continues in "gorge-ous" scenery, passing under a massive rockhouse with a huge overhang at 1.8 miles. Weave among boulders and along a cliffline, culminating in a trip under a rockfall arch at 1.9 miles. At 2.2 miles, Trail #2 leaves right. Keep straight, soon leaving the state park boundaries for the Daniel Boone National Forest. At 2.5 miles, reach a delicate 10-foot curtain-type fall that drops just uptrail, Veil Cascade.

Then the Trace follows steps to another river beach, curving on a big bend in the Cumberland. Reach a wooden bridge crossing Catfish Creek at 2.9 miles. Look upstream for Catfish Creek Cascades, pouring a dozen feet over a rock face then zig zagging amid boulders before flowing under the bridge upon which you stand.

This bridge roughly marks your entrance into the Daniel Boone National Forest. Keep downriver, closer to the water. Dance among big boulders to enter the Dog Slaughter Creek valley and a trail junction at 3.3 miles. Here, take the Dog Slaughter Trail leaving right. This fascinating path winds among big rocks and along rockhouses to reach Dog Slaughter Falls at 3.5 miles. Dog Slaughter Falls makes a wide, curtain-type drop of 20 feet into a big plunge pool, not as powerful as Cumberland Falls but a sight to see in its own right.

Mileages
0.0   Cumberland Falls trailhead
0.3   Lovers Leap overlook
0.7   Eagle Falls view
1.1   Rock House Falls
1.6   Anvil Falls
2.2   Trail 2 leaves right
2.5   Veil Cascade
2.9   Catfish Creek Cascades
3.2   Right on Dog Slaughter Falls Trail
3.5   Dog Slaughter Falls
7.0   Cumberland Falls trailhead

EAGLE FALLS CUMBERLAND FALLS

Hike Summary: This is a "must-do" hike, featuring rumbling Cumberland Falls and regal Eagle Falls, along with vistas of the Cumberland River and the gorge below Cumberland Falls. Leave the trailhead to see huge rumbling 65-foot Cumberland Falls, a river-wide horseshoe cataract of power, mist and glory. Walk along bluffs above the Cumberland River before traipsing among boulder-strewn bottoms to visit 40-foot Eagle Falls. Work up Eagle Creek, passing Eagle Creek Cascades and wooded hills. Make a loop then take a side trail to an overlook of the Cumberland River from on high.

DISTANCE: 2.2-mile balloon loop
HIKING TIME: 1.5 hours
DIFFICULTY: Moderate
HIGHLIGHTS: Cumberland Falls, Eagle Falls, Eagle Creek Cascades, overlooks
CAUTIONS: Steep terrain, irregular segments of trail
FEES/PERMITS: No fees or permits required
OTHER TRAIL USERS: None
TRAIL CONTACTS: Cumberland Falls State Resort Park, 7351 Highway 90, Corbin, KY 40701, (606) 528-4121, http://parks.ky.gov/parks/resortparks/cumberland-falls/

Finding the trailhead: From Exit 25 on I-75 near Corbin, take US 25W south for 7.5 miles to KY 90. Turn right and take KY 90 west for 8.4 miles, bridging the Cumberland River just above Cumberland Falls. From the bridge continue on KY 90 for .3 mile farther to

reach the Eagle Falls trailhead on your right. GPS Trailhead Coordinates: N36° 50.210′, W84° 20.733′

What an exciting hike, from the first step to the last! And for a 2.2-mile hike it is somewhat strenuous—lots of ups and downs, steps, staircases, bouldery bottoms and hills. However, the short overall distance gives it a moderate rating. Nevertheless, it can be done by anyone taking his or

her time. Moreover, you will want to take your time, snapping pictures and recording videos.

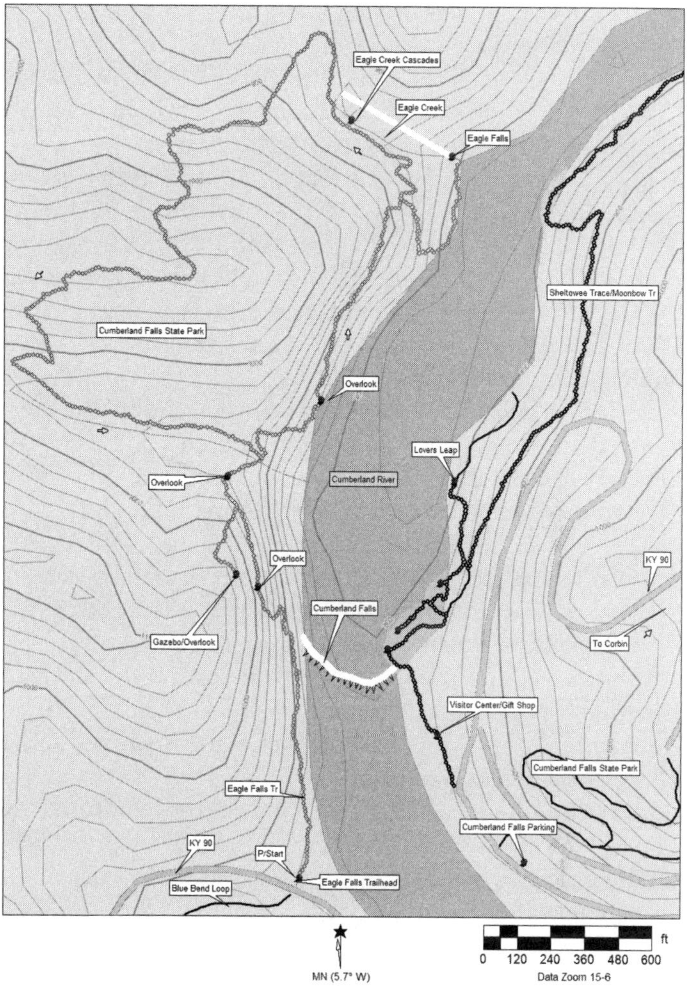

Leave the Eagle Falls trailhead, quickly come alongside the Cumberland River. The awesome roar of Cumberland Falls can already be heard. Signs warn against coming too close to the river. Someone might be swept over the falls. It has happened. Come along a dripping cliffline and dripping bluff at .1 mile. Climb well above the falls. At .2 mile, squeeze under an overhanging rock then gain an open downriver vista, below Cumberland Falls.

At .3 mile, reach the spur to the gorge overlook. Save that for later. Continue on the Eagle Falls Trail, dipping to a hollow and along an echoing cliffline where views open upriver of massive Cumberland Falls, making its 65-foot high, 125-foot wide vertical dive over rock, crashing in whirling mist. No wonder it is called the Niagara of the South. You can also see much of the state park facilities across the river. At .4 mile, step over a creek and meet a trail intersection, reaching the loop portion of the Eagle Falls Trail. Stay right here, running parallel to the Cumberland River. Continue through woods, gaining river views to make another trail intersection at .6 mile. Turn right here toward Eagle Falls. Stone, wood, and metal steps lead down toward the curtain-type spiller. A metal stairway dips amid massive boulders and the riparian bottoms along the Cumberland River. Sand, boulders and vegetation mix as you pick your way downstream in the bottoms. The going is slow.

Then, at .7 mile, reach 40-foot Eagle Falls. Here, Eagle Creek dives off a horizontal stone rim, splashing into a rock-strewn pool. Boulders of all sizes contrast with the white falling water and the bubble-topped pool. Eagle Creek flows a bit more through more boulders before making a final much shorter drop into the Cumberland River. The plentitude of rocks near Eagle Falls allow scramblers to gain a multitude of perches from which to view the spiller. Hikers can also access a beach along the Cumberland River.

Backtrack from Eagle Falls then resume the loop. Come back alongside Eagle Creek then turn up the waterway amid mosses, ferns and rhododendron. At .9 mile, reach Eagle Creek Cascades. Here, Eagle Creek makes a 10-foot sloped slide over flat rock, ending in a short vertical drop. Note how Eagle Creek makes a sharp bend to the left just below Eagle Creek Cascades.

The trail proceeds beyond this second spiller, curving with the curve of Eagle Creek before climbing away from the water altogether, passing an overhang with much stone debris at its bottom at 1.1 miles. Top out on an unnamed ridge at 1.3 miles. Enjoy a brief level spell amid xeric woods before dropping again. Come alongside a tributary of the Cumberland River at 1.5 miles. Roll down the evergreen rich hollow, completing the loop portion of the hike at 1.7 miles. From here, backtrack, climbing to an intersection at 1.8 miles. Head right here, ascending a host of wooden steps, topping out on a fence-bordered ledge. Here stands a wooden gazebo built in the 1930s by the Civilian Conservation Corps (CCC), a government works organization used to employ young men during the Great Depression. The CCC developed many of the trails and facilities here at

Cumberland Falls and this gazebo stands proud from that era. From this cliffline you can look down on the gorge through which the Cumberland River flows. It is a backtrack from this point, and you return to the Eagle Falls trailhead at 2.2 miles.

Mileages

0.0	Eagle Falls trailhead
0.4	Begin loop portion of hike
0.6	Spur to Eagle Falls
0.7	Eagle Falls
0.9	Eagle Creek Cascade
1.7	Finish loop portion of hike
2.2	Eagle Falls trailhead

BLUE BEND LOOP

Hike Summary: This circuit hike offers a little bit of everything. Start out on the historic wagon road that once accessed Cumberland Falls before heading deep into a state nature preserve. Enjoy the wealth of protected flora and fauna as well as old homesites before dropping to the Cumberland River and hiking the one and only Sheltowee Trace. Cruise through boulders and bottomland along the Kentucky wild river. Pass waterside boulders perfect for relaxing. Blue Bend Falls, a low flow cascade, is another highlight. The final part of the hike leads along KY 90, then you are back at the trailhead. The trail is in good shape and much of it offers easy walking.

DISTANCE: 4.6-mile loop
HIKING TIME: 2.1 hours
DIFFICULTY: Moderate
HIGHLIGHTS: Cumberland Falls State Park Nature Preserve, Blue Bend Falls, river views
CAUTIONS: None
FEES/PERMITS: No fees or permits required
OTHER TRAIL USERS: None
TRAIL CONTACTS: Cumberland Falls State Park, 7351 Highway 90, Corbin, KY 40701, (606) 528-4121, http://parks.ky.gov/parks/resortparks/cumberland-falls/

Finding the trailhead: From Exit 25 on I-75 near Corbin, take US 25W south for 7.5 miles to KY 90. Turn right and take KY 90 west

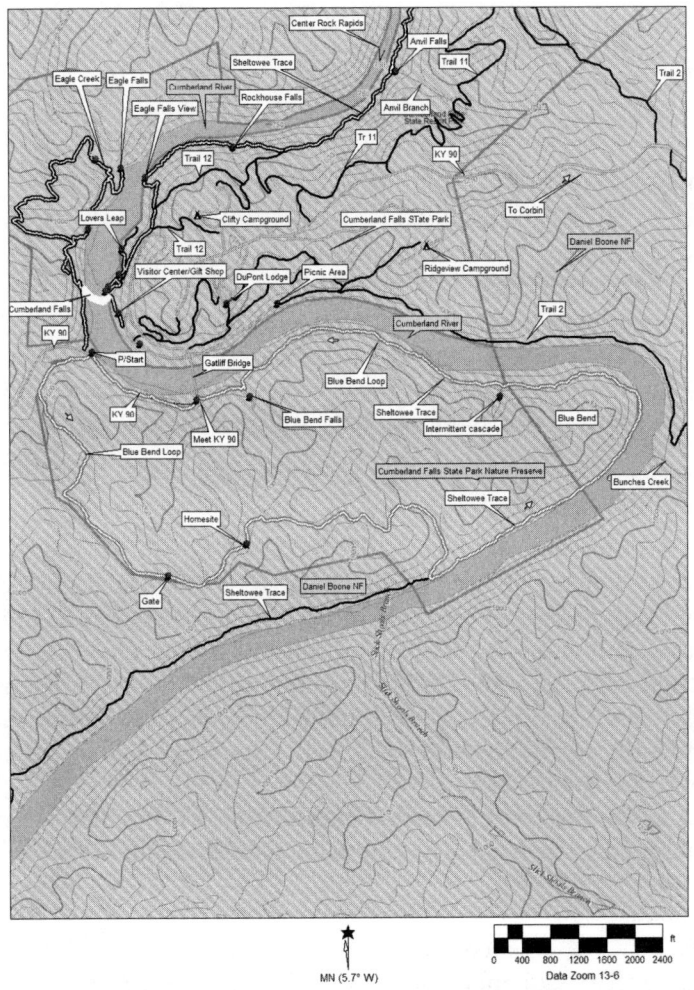

for 8.4 miles, bridging the Cumberland River just above Cumberland Falls. From the bridge continue on KY 90 for .3 mile farther to reach the Eagle Falls trailhead on your right. The Blue Bend Trail starts on the south side of KY 90, away from the Cumberland River. GPS Trailhead Coordinates: N36° 50.210', W84° 20.733'

This loop explores the lesser visited side of Cumberland Falls State Park and the adjoining eponymous Kentucky nature preserve. Numerous rockhouses, boulders, water features, flora and fauna are protected within the 1,294-acre preserve. Leave KY 90 on a crumbling asphalt track rising

away from the Cumberland River. The Blue Bend Loop shortly leaves the asphalt track left on stone steps to join an older roadbed. This track was the wagon route visitors used to reach Cumberland Falls after getting off the train at the hamlet of Parkers Lake, along what is now US 27. Imagine their excitement while descending to the Cumberland River and first hearing the roar of the falls!

Our excitement is lesser as we are climbing through woods away from the falls, soon turning away from KY 90. Hemlock and rhododendron crowd the path. Briefly jump off the wagon track, working around an eroded segment before rejoining the track and coming to a trail sign at .5 mile. You have just climbed nearly 300 feet. Here, the Blue Bend Loop splits away from the old wagon road and turns left, following a foot-friendly doubletrack trail heading southeast. Ramble along the ridge in hardwoods, holly and shortleaf pine. At .9 mile, walk through a long-disused metal gate. White oaks rise high in these woods.

At 1.2 miles, the Blue Bend Loop reaches a homesite on a level spot in the ridgeline. Jonquils still bloom here in early spring, and the crumbling rock foundation is a living relic of a forgotten Kentuckian who welcomed the season of renewal. Ahead, look for evidence of more homesites or farmed land, such as wolf trees. These trees, obviously much larger than those of the surrounding forest, were once "lone wolves"—a white oak that once shaded a home, for example, or a tree in a grazing pasture. These trees typically have thick trunks and horizontal or outward-protruding branches. Since the park's inception, a forest has grown around these wolf trees. They are no longer alone, but they do stand out.

At 1.7 miles, the Blue Bend Loop turns into a hollow and begins diving for the Cumberland River. The hollow opens the way to the Cumberland River. Ironically, this segment of the mighty Cumberland is flowing nearly silently, belying the river's big fall just two miles downstream. Pass near a small sandstone rockhouse just before meeting the Sheltowee Trace at 2.1 miles. Here, turn left, following Kentucky's master path downstream in bottoms rich with beard cane, pawpaw and tulip trees, as well as wildflowers aplenty in spring. River birch and sycamore claim the terrain closest to the river.

By 2.7 miles, the flat has narrowed, with bluffs to your left and the river to your right. Bunches Creek enters the waterway across the river. You are making the big westerly curve around Blue Bend. The footing isn't bad. Occasional small branches trickle across the path. Watch for outcrops stretching into the river where you can look on the water. Ahead, the Sheltowee Trace saddles along rock palisades. At 3.1 miles, the trail squeezes between the bluff and a fallen boulder. At 3.3 miles, the trail crosses a small streamlet with a dripping cascade falling from a bluff back from the trail. This stream can dry up in late summer and fall.

The beauty grows with every step. The Cumberland starts creating noisy rapids. At 3.9 miles, meet a stone state park boundary marker. Deciduous magnolias grow in profusion. At 4.1 miles, reach a hiker bridge over a creek and Blue Bend Falls. Here, a user created trail leads upstream from the hiker bridge to Blue Bend Falls. This low-flow spiller is best enjoyed in spring when you can see it pour 26 feet over a two-layered rock ledge into a crumbled stone pile then gather itself to become a small creek and flow on to the Cumberland River.

The Sheltowee Trace climbs from Blue Bend Falls then drops back to reach Gatliff Bridge and KY 90. From here, carefully walk along the two lane paved road for .3 mile, returning to the Eagle Falls trailhead at 4.6 miles.

Mileages

0.0	Eagle Falls trailhead
0.5	Leave historic wagon road
2.1	Left on Sheltowee Trace
3.3	Low flow cascade
4.1	Blue Bend Falls
4.6	Eagle Falls trailhead

NATURAL ARCH SCENIC AREA AND LOOP

Hike Summary: Visit one of Daniel Boone National Forest's designated scenic areas on this trek. First, walk a quarter-mile to view massive Natural Arch, a bridge-like sandstone span rising above the forest. Next hike to a closer view of the arch then join the Buffalo Valley Loop, making a circuit, where you pass directly beneath Natural Arch, then along cool, dark tributaries. Next, rise to pass a second lesser-visited arch known as the Big Cutoff. Plan to make a day of your adventure, enjoying the grounds of the fine day use area at the trailhead, including two picnic shelters.

DISTANCE: .5 mile there and back plus 6.0-mile loop
HIKING TIME: 3.5 hours
DIFFICULTY: Moderate
HIGHLIGHTS: Views of Natural Arch, Natural Arch, Big Cutoff Arch
CAUTIONS: None
FEES/PERMITS: Parking fee required
OTHER TRAIL USERS: None
TRAIL CONTACTS: Daniel Boone National Forest, Stearns Ranger District, 3320 US 27 North, Whitley City, KY 42653, (606)376-5323, www.fs.usda.gov/dbnf

Finding the trailhead: From the Stearns Rangers Station on US 27 a little north of Whitley City, take US 27 north for 4.5 miles and turn left on Day Ridge Road, KY 927. Follow KY 927 west for 1.8 miles then turn right into the Natural Arch Scenic Area. Ahead, keep straight to reach the parking area by the overlook trail. GPS Trailhead Coordinates: N36° 50.464', W84° 30.733'

The Daniel Boone National Forest has made Natural Arch Scenic Area one of its "go to" destinations, and developed the trailhead in fine fashion. Parking and picnicking places are ample and the trails are in fine shape. Your first order of business should be to hike the .25-mile trail to

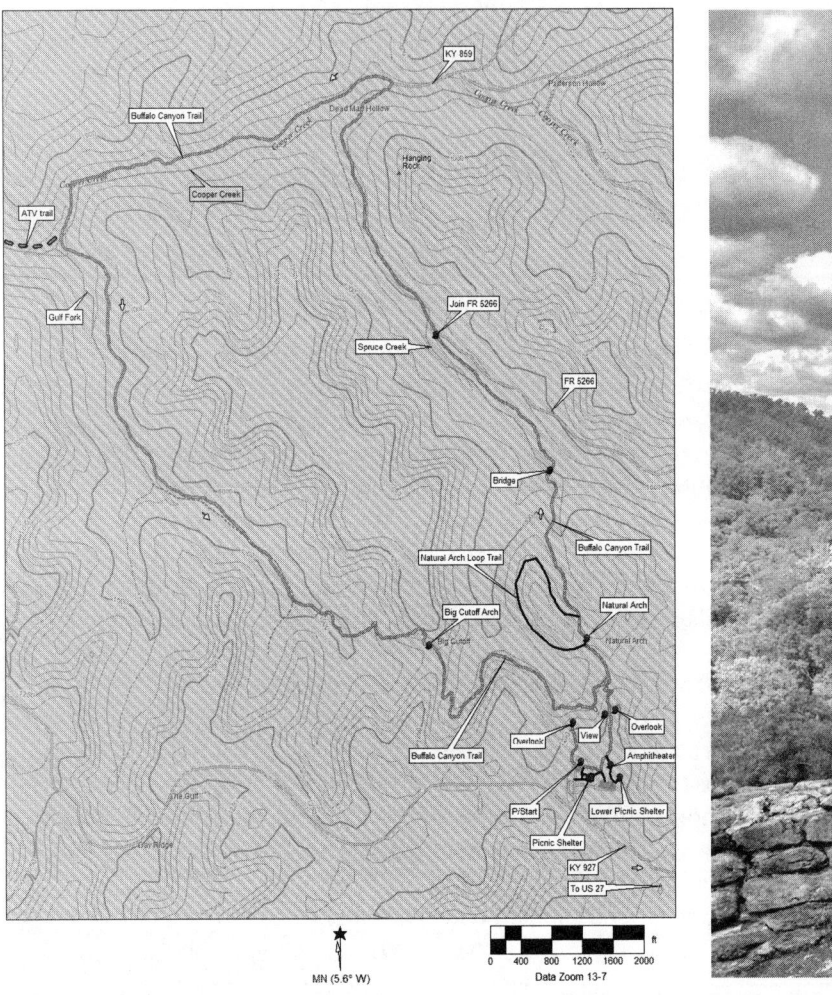

the overlook of Natural Arch. After returning from the overlook, embark on the loop hike, first viewing Natural Arch from a sandstone flat, then visiting massive Natural Arch, home to aboriginal Kentuckians. This stone bridge is one of the largest in southern Kentucky. From there, you can then make the circuit using the Buffalo Canyon Trail.

To start your hike from the upper parking area, join the concrete path leading west then north, descending to a veranda-like overlook with interpretive information and benches. Natural Arch stands in the fore while other stone features above the woodlands. Here, you can appreci-

ate the massive size of the stone bridge and the lands through which you are going to hike.

Backtrack to the parking area, then head east toward the amphitheater. Leave the concrete walkways of the picnic area, joining the Natural Arch Loop Trail. The asphalt trail leads into a gorgeous area, passing a pair of overlooks that are among the finest vistas in the Bluegrass State. After soaking in a dead on view of Natural Arch from an open stone slab, descend stone steps aplenty amid stone formations. At .8 mile (this distance includes the .5 mile there and back on the overlook trail) reach the loop portion of the hike. Stay right toward Natural Arch, reaching another intersection at .9 mile. Here, the Natural Arch Loop Trail circles the base of the sandstone uplift that is Natural Arch.

Our hike stays right, climbing carved naked rock to immediately pass under the 60 feet high and 100 feet wide stone bridge. The hike then leads along an enormous fenced off archeologically rich rock shelter bordering Natural Arch. Natives called this home and the locale has been thoroughly exhumed.

Ahead, reach the other end of the mile-long Natural Arch Loop Trail (which makes an agreeable hike of its own) then descend on lesser-used pathway, officially joining the Buffalo Canyon Trail. Descend along a streamlet featuring wet-weather cascades. At 1.4 miles, bridge Spruce Branch and continue down along evergreen darkened stream corridor.

The valley widens and the Buffalo Canyon Trail emerges onto FR 5266 at 1.9 miles. Here, join the quiet gravel track, continuing down the Spruce Branch valley. Work around a private inholding. Curve down to Cooper Creek, reaching a low water crossing at 2.6 miles. Concrete blocks rise above the crossing at low water levels and serve as stepping stones. Once across, head left, downstream along Cooper Creek, following a doubletrack (KY 859 leads right). ATVs use this part of the trail, creating mud holes in places. Nevertheless, the scenery is outstanding as Cooper Creek flows in shoals and pools under deep green woods.

At 3.5 miles, the trail crosses over to the left bank. At 3.6 miles, the ATV track splits right while the Buffalo Canyon Trail turns left up Gulf Fork. Begin ascending Gulf Fork hollow, along a side slope above the stream. Cross occasional feeder streams of Gulf Fork. Note the preponderance of beech trees here. Beechnuts are an important food for wildlife. This valley is good for spring wildflowers, too.

Turn up a fork of Gulf Fork, criss-crossing the small stream a few times before climbing away at 4.9 miles. By 5.2 miles, you have risen to saddle along a colossal cliffline rising overhead. Look left for the lesser visited Big Cutoff Arch to the left of the trail, where the cliffline has eroded through. This is technically an arch but it doesn't get the style points that does Natural Arch, since this arch seems more a hole or window in the cliffline, which is essentially is, spanning about 20' x 20'. Nevertheless, walk up and through the arch. Steep and narrow passages extend both ways to lands above.

Climb away from the arch, only to join another cliffline. Cruise beneath this rock wall to complete the loop at 6.2 miles. From here, climb the steps away from Natural Arch and back toward the day use area, completing the trek at 6.5 miles.

Mileages

0.0	Leave Natural Bridge parking area for overlook
0.5	Head toward Natural Arch after leaving parking area a second time
0.8	Right toward Natural Arch
0.9	Right again, pass under Natural Arch
1.4	Bridge Spruce Branch
1.9	Left on FR 5266
2.6	Cross Cooper Creek, turn left
3.6	Left up Gulf Fork
4.9	Leave stream
5.2	Cliffline, Big Cutoff Arch
6.2	Complete loop, backtrack
6.5	Return to Natural Bridge parking area

NORTH FORK BIG CREEK FALLS

Hike Summary: This adventure takes hikers along the Sheltowee Trace from a trailhead on US 27 under a hardwood forest then cuts through a slice of civilization before returning to national forest land. Here, you descend into North Fork Big Creek vale where the trees rise tall. North Fork flows alongside the path. The trail then continues atop a cliffline before finding a break and curving into an incredible semi-circular rockhouse mixed with big boulders and highlighted by North Fork Big Creek Falls, a spiller that pours directly from atop the rockhouse.

DISTANCE: 4.8-mile there-and-back
HIKING TIME: 2.3 hours
DIFFICULTY: Easy-moderate
HIGHLIGHTS: North Fork Big Creek Falls, enormous and unusual rockhouse
CAUTIONS: Road crossings
FEES/PERMITS: No fees or permits required
OTHER TRAIL USERS: Equestrians on first part of hike
TRAIL CONTACTS: Daniel Boone National Forest, Stearns Ranger District, 3320 US 27 North, Whitley City, KY 42653, (606)376-5323, www.fs.usda.gov/dbnf

Finding the trailhead: From the Stearns District Ranger Station on US 27 just north of Whitley City, take US 27 north for 1.1 miles to

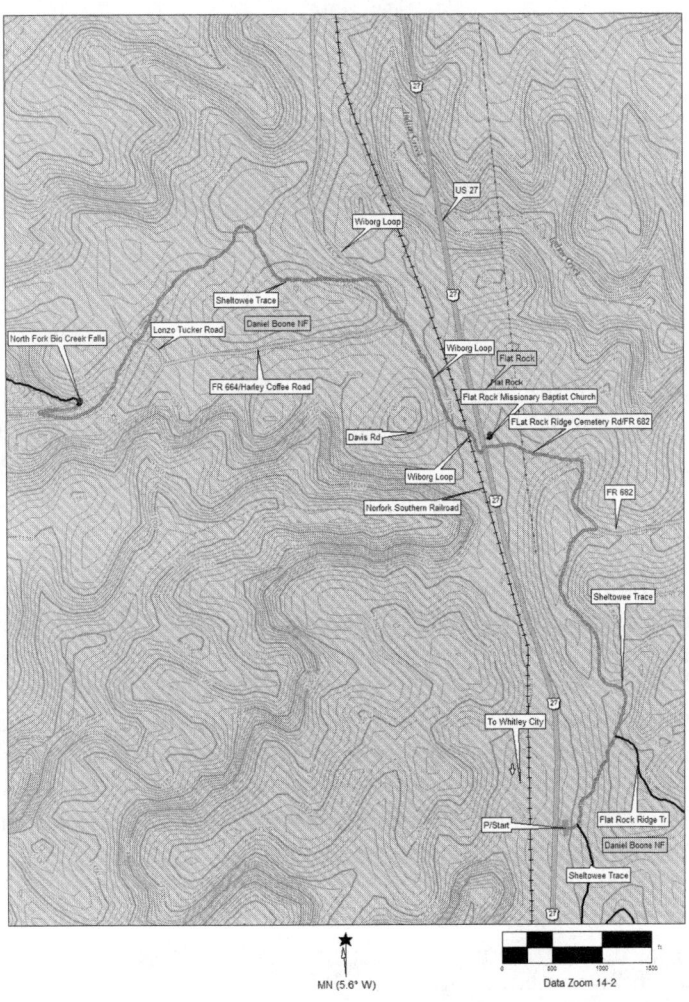

reach the Sheltowee Trace parking area on your right, the east side of US 27. GPS Trailhead Coordinates: N36° 47.101′, W84° 28.911′

This hike is a bit unusual as it rambles through the Daniel Boone National Forest, then wanders through civilization for a bit before returning to national forest land to view a major highlight that is not only North Fork Big Creek Falls, but the surrounding rockhouse into which it flows. The remarkable rockhouse is very large and very deep, almost "V" shaped. The falls drops at the base of the "V." In front of the rock-

house stand gigantic fallen boulders. It seems the boulders were once part of the greater rockhouse that partially collapsed. The Sheltowee Trace takes you directly into and around the back of the shelter, delivering a view of the falls from multiple directions. Be forewarned, in late summer and autumn this fall can nearly dry up.

Even though you have multiple trail intersections and a short road walk, the hike is mostly easy. Elevation changes are less than 200 feet. The trek leaves the US 27 trailhead. Here, walk just a few feet under a powerline clearing and reach a trail junction. Head left with the

Sheltowee Trace, southbound toward Yahoo Falls, though this immediate stretch of the Trace is heading north. Enter woods of white oak, hickory and maple on an easy level path.

At .2 mile, come to another trail intersection. Here, the Flat Rock Ridge Trail leaves right for Railroad Fork. Stay left here with the Sheltowee Trace, northbound. Cut back under the powerline at .3 mile then come to the edge of national forest land. Emerge onto Forest Road 682 at .7 mile. Turn left, west, on FR 682. At .9 mile, the forest road becomes paved and the name changes to Flat Rock Ridge Cemetery Road. Continue on the paved road and at 1.0 mile meet US 27 at Flat Rock Missionary Baptist Church.

Cross US 27 and pick up paved Wiborg Loop. Follow it northwest to cross the Norfolk Southern Railroad track. Walk Wiborg Loop beyond some houses to reach the intersection of Wiborg Loop and Harley Coffee Road at 1.3 miles. Here, the Sheltowee Trace reenters woods and national forest land. Such road walks are necessary on a long trail such as the Sheltowee Trace (or Appalachian Trail) simply because it is impossible to find hundreds of contiguous miles of public lands on which to place a trail without road walks amid tracts of private property.

Rise back into the national forest. Curve west at 1.5 miles, staying with the plastic blazes emblazoned with the turtle on them, the Sheltowee Trace's official moniker. This path was the 100th designated federal national recreation trail, dedicated in June of 1979. The trail is named in honor of Daniel Boone, Kentucky's famed pioneer. Sheltowee, meaning Big Turtle, was the name given to Boone after he was adopted into the Shawnee tribe as the son of the great war chief Blackfish. Earlier, while being pursued by the Shawnee, Boone hid beneath the waters of a creek, breathing through a reed "straw," thus earning his nickname. Hikers who tread this trail will be "following the turtle."

At 1.7 miles, don't miss the left turn into the North Fork Big Creek watershed. The trailside creek starts picking up steam as you descend. If the stream is flowing boldly at this point the falls will be exciting, if not, the falls may be but a trickle. At 2.0 miles, step over a small tributary coming in on your left. Cross paved Lonzo Tucker Road at 2.1 miles. The gorge of North Fork drops off well below as the Sheltowee Trace stays atop a cliffline. Find a crevice in the cliffline then curve back along the base of the cliffline, aiming for North Fork. The Sheltowee Trace comes to then runs under a colossal rockhouse fronted by a boulder jumble. The splatter of North Fork Big Creek Falls echoes off the rock and you come to the spiller at 2.4 miles. Here, at the deepest cleft in the rockhouse, North Fork Big Creek is following gravity's orders and dropping 30 or so feet from the top of the rockhouse, then re-forms and flows under the boulder jumble just outside the rockhouse. It's another show of geological and aquatic beauty in Kentucky's Daniel Boone National Forest.

Mileages
0.0   US 27 trailhead
0.7   Leave on FR 682
1.0   Cross US 27
1.3   Reenter national forest land
2.4   North Fork Big Creek Falls
4.8   US 27 trailhead

BARREN FORK HERITAGE TRAIL

Hike Summary: This concrete all-accessible trail makes a short loop through what once was the heart of an early Kentucky coal mining camp. Barren Fork Coal Camp, in operation for over 5 decades, stood on the site. It was ultimately purchased by the Daniel Boone National Forest. Forest personnel developed an accessible trail complemented with interpretive signage detailing

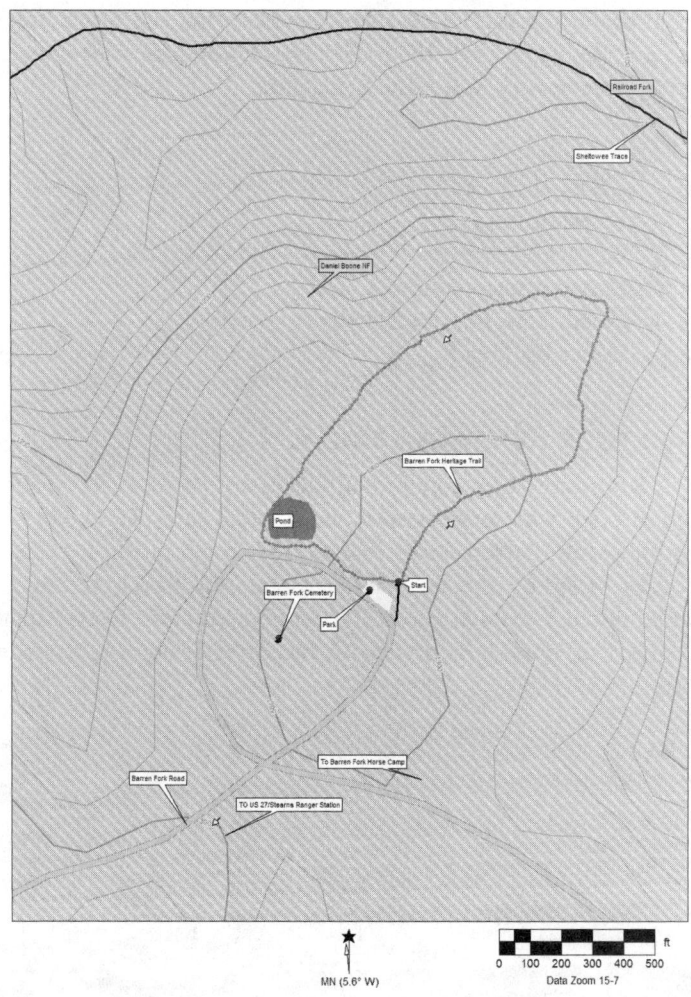

life at this locale, now listed on the National Register of Historic Places. Today you can explore the site and its relics as well as the adjacent cemetery, learning about a Bluegrass State lifeway now lost to time.

DISTANCE: .6-mile all access loop
HIKING TIME: .5 hour
DIFFICULTY: Easy
HIGHLIGHTS: Relics of Barren Fork Coal Camp,
    interpretive information

CAUTIONS: None
FEES/PERMITS: No fees or permits required
OTHER TRAIL USERS: Wheelchair hikers
TRAIL CONTACTS: Daniel Boone National Forest, Stearns Ranger District, 3320 US 27 North, Whitley City, KY 42653, (606)376-5323, www.fs.usda.gov/dbnf

Finding the trailhead: From the Stearns Ranger Station on US 27 just north of Whitely City, take paved Forest Road 684 east for .7 mile, then stay left toward the Barren Fork Cemetery as FR 684 splits right toward Barren Fork Horse Camp. The trailhead is just ahead, next to Barren Fork Cemetery. GPS Trailhead Coordinates: N36° 46.645', W84° 28.095'

Kentucky is known as a coal producing state and has been that way for over a century and a half. Coal producing on a mass scale started here in eastern Kentucky when a railroad line was laid from Cincinnati to near Whitley City in the 1870s, allowing mass produced coal a way to market. The Barren Fork drainage was purchased by what became Barren Fork Mining and Coal Company. A private rail line was laid along what become known as Railroad Fork. Local farmers and some folks from adjacent states were hired and brought to the remote location.

Being in the back of beyond, the coal company built a community for them to live and work along Railroad Fork, a regular company town. The company-owned houses were modest, mostly a few rooms with a porch, without running water or indoor plumbing, but residents could tie into the electrical grid of the coal company. That perk alone was a major attractor for hiring men from their independent self-sustaining farms to the subservient company way of life. These communities grew overnight.

The mining area consisted of several shafts along Railroad Fork, working a coal seam stretching for 3 miles. The coal tipple rose above the scene, where the black nuggets were separated and graded out before being run up an incline to the waiting railroad line, where they were dumped into open cars.

The company town also included a schoolhouse, post office, a church and a company store. They even had a baseball field. Social gatherings were held under rockhouses along Railroad Fork. The workers were paid in scrip they could use to purchase goods at the company store. Often, the workers used up all their earnings in scrip before the month was over, and thus were not due a cash balance from the mining company. This was a case of "too much month at the end of the money."

In 1912, the coal camp was moved from the flats along Railroad Fork up to the ridgetop location where the Barren Fork Heritage Trail runs. Over 40 homes were located up here, along with the coal processing center. Not only miners lived here. Others came to work servicing the mining community, from carpenters to build for the camp, managers and stock boys to operate the company store to laundresses washing the clothes. Most preachers during this time were circuit riders, going from church to church each Sunday, filling the pulpit at least once a month.

By the 1920s, the coal supply was expanding and the coal price dwindling. Then the combination of the Great Depression and Kentucky's coal miners attempting to unionize squeezed out any potential profit margin. After five decades of mining on Barren Fork, in the year 1935 the workers at Barren Fork Mine voted to unionize. The owners of the mine decided to close the mine instead.

The end of the community came as quickly as Barren Fork had sprung up. Many miners moved out and in 1936 the United States Forest Service bought the land and the coal operation lock, stock and barrel, selling off all the useable mining equipment. Interestingly, some mining families hung on in their rented homes for a few years before moving on to greener pastures. Time passed and the forest regenerated, covering up most of a town that bustled for 5 decades.

Today, you can walk the interpretive trail and learn more about this community. Though time and regrowth has obliterated much of the hamlet, building foundations and squared off parcels of land can still be seen, especially during winter and spring, before leaf out. You can also see the pond that was used for water. Barren Fork Cemetery is maintained to this day. Many descendants of the coal miners still live in McCreary County and Whitley City. Along with these locals you can reflect on Kentucky's coal heritage, protected here as yet another unique parcel of the Daniel Boone National Forest. If you want to see more relics of the Barren Fork mining industry take the Sheltowee Trace northbound from the US 27 trailhead just north of the Stearns Ranger Station. The first 3.5 miles travel past old mines and seams along the very railroad grade used by the engines that served Barren Fork Mining and Coal Company.

Mileages
0.0   Barren Fork Heritage Trail parking
0.7   Barren Fork Heritage Trail parking

YAHOO FALLS YAHOO ARCH

Hike Summary: This walk explores Kentucky's highest cataract—Yahoo Falls—as well as an overlook of the Big South Fork and fascinating Yahoo Arch, a geological feature you can view from afar, from below and from above. It all starts at the Big South Fork National River and Recreation Area's Yahoo Falls Scenic Area, where you enter a nest of trails delivering multiple vantages of Yahoo Falls before crossing into the Daniel Boone National Forest, where Yahoo Arch awaits, and a concentration of geological wonderment.

DISTANCE: 2.8-mile loop with spur
HIKING TIME: 1.8 hours
DIFFICULTY: Easy
HIGHLIGHTS: Yahoo Falls, Roaring Rocks Cataract, rock shelters, boulder passages, Yahoo Arch
CAUTIONS: Maze of trails around Yahoo Falls
FEES/PERMITS: No fees or permits required
OTHER TRAIL USERS: None
TRAIL CONTACTS: Daniel Boone National Forest, Stearns Ranger District, 3320 US 27 North, Whitley City, KY 42653, (606)376-5323, www.fs.usda.gov/dbnf

Finding the trailhead: From the intersection of KY 700 and US 27 just north of Whitely City, take KY 700 west for 3.9 miles to turn right onto Yahoo Falls Road. Follow it for 1.5 miles to reach a restroom and parking area for Yahoo Falls at the lower end of the parking area loop road. The trail starts on your right. GPS Trailhead Coordinates: N36° 46.424', W84° 31.455'

Visitors to Yahoo Falls Scenic Area have become lost for days in the maze of trails around Yahoo Falls. Not really, but people do get mighty confused among the many intersections. Study the map in this guide, then take a picture of the trailhead map with your phone and your chance of staying found will greatly increase. These nature trails do take you to the wealth of highlights around here and are well worth the possibility of getting turned around.

Leave the trailhead on the signed path toward Yahoo Falls. Soon take the short spur left to an overlook of the Big South Fork as it makes a bend at the confluence with Yahoo Creek. This part of the river can be backed up as part of Lake Cumberland when water levels are high.

148 | SOUTHERN DANIEL BOONE NATIONAL FOREST

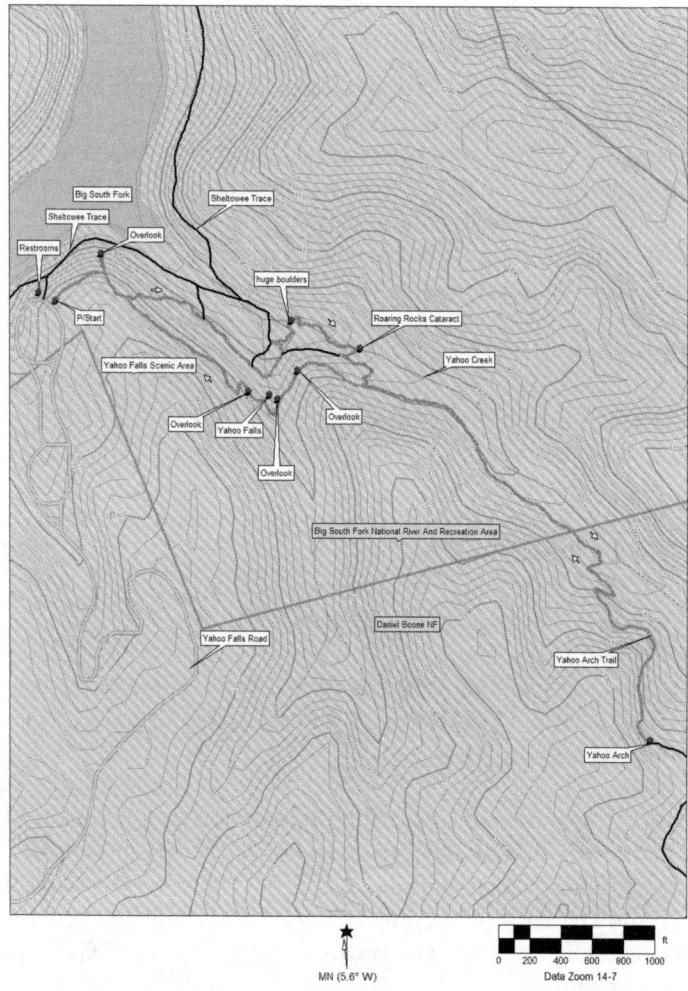

At .2 mile, reach an intersection. Head left here toward the base of Yahoo Falls. Soon, a long set of metal stairs lead you below a steep cliffline. At .3 mile pass a spur leading left to the Sheltowee Trace but stay straight, running along the base of the daunting cliffline you just descended via metal stairs. As you trek forward the water song of Yahoo Falls drifts into your ears while Yahoo Creek gurgles amid a riot of greenery below.

Reach Yahoo Falls at .4 mile. Here, Kentucky's highest waterfall plummets 113 feet from a stone ledge undercut with one of the biggest rockhouses around. This massive shelter was used by aboriginal Kentuckians

for time untold. The main trail circles behind Yahoo Falls while steps lead to the base of Yahoo Falls. The enormity of the shelter and height of the falls create yet another noteworthy Bluegrass spectacle.

After circling behind Yahoo Falls and around the archeological rich rockhouse, head left at an intersection, descending away from the cliffline. A short switchback leads you to still another intersection. The trail leading left bridges the creek of Yahoo Falls. However, we turn right up the actual Yahoo Creek. The trail seems to dead end at some monstrous boulders but you follow the creek upstream, squeezing either through or around the boulders.

The trail re-forms beyond the boulders and you continue upstream criss-crossing Yahoo Creek. Reach Roaring Rocks Cataract at .6 mile. This narrow spigot-like falls rushes 30 or so feet through a boulder garden. Unfortunately, most of the spindly cataract is screened by rhododendron, with the lowermost portion viewable.

The highlight reel continues as we cross Yahoo Creek one last time then climb back to a cliffline. Hopefully you have successfully navigated the trail maze this far. Here, head left toward Yahoo Arch. This is the out-and-back part of the hike. Continue up the valley of Yahoo Creek, soon entering the Daniel Boone National Forest. Switchbacks help you gain ground, then join a formidable cliffline and very deep rockhouse at 1.5 miles. Just when you move on after admiring this geological feature Yahoo Arch rises in all its glory. Here, the arch stands 17 feet at its highest and 70 feet in length. The trail goes directly under the arch and when you look back you will see a smaller window arch, four feet high, on the right of the primary arch—an arch within an arch.

Explore Yahoo Arch from all angles. Walk atop the stone bridge. Interestingly, despite the relatively thin deck of the arch trees grow atop it, spreading their roots wide to grasp the shallow soil. While up here you will also see a secondary upper rockhouse adjacent to Yahoo Arch, a dry shelter undoubtedly used by aboriginals. This is clearly a locale of geological significance in the Daniel Boone National Forest.

The thrills are not over yet. Backtrack .8 mile then keep straight at the intersection to observe Yahoo Falls from above the cliffline. You will pass 2 designated overlooks then cross the unnamed creek of Yahoo Falls just above the cataract. Pass a third and final up top overlook, then continue back toward the parking area, completing the hike at 2.8 miles. While here, consider a picnic, as the scenic area features several picnic tables. Also you can explore the Big South Fork River as well as a segment of Kentucky's master path, the Sheltowee Trace.

Mileages

0.0	Yahoo Falls parking area
0.2	Left at intersection after visiting overlook, descend stairs
0.4	Yahoo Falls
0.6	Roaring Rocks Cataract
1.5	Yahoo Arch, backtrack
2.3	Rejoin loop, pass 3 overlooks above Yahoo Falls
2.8	Yahoo Falls parking area

MARKERS ARCH YAHOO ARCH

Hike Summary: The hike visits two natural arches located near one another in the southern end of the Daniel Boone National Forest. The first part of the hike travels a nearly level ridge before dropping into the Yahoo Creek watershed, where you find Yahoo Arch and adjacent rockhouses below the cliffline. Explore the arch from all angles then backtrack to the Markers Arch Trail. This path leads through uplands before dropping toward upper Yahoo Creek where this second natural bridge makes its span.

DISTANCE: 2.6-miles in two out-and-back hikes from one trailhead
HIKING TIME: 1.5 hours
DIFFICULTY: Easy
HIGHLIGHTS: Yahoo Arch, Markers Arch
CAUTIONS: None
FEES/PERMITS: No fees or permits required
OTHER TRAIL USERS: None
TRAIL CONTACTS: Daniel Boone National Forest, Stearns Ranger District, 3320 US 27 North, Whitley City, KY 42653, (606)376-5323, www.fs.usda.gov/dbnf

Finding the trailhead: From the intersection of KY 700 and US 27 just north of Whitely City, take KY 700 west for 2.9 miles to the signed trailhead on your right. GPS Trailhead Coordinates: N36° 45.403', W84° 30.718'

This easy hike allows you to bag two arches in one visit, from a lesser used trailhead. Your first conquest will be Yahoo Arch, 70 feet long and 17 feet high. This is one of hundreds of arches in the Daniel Boone National Forest. The Red River Gorge alone has more than 100 arches. It is generally

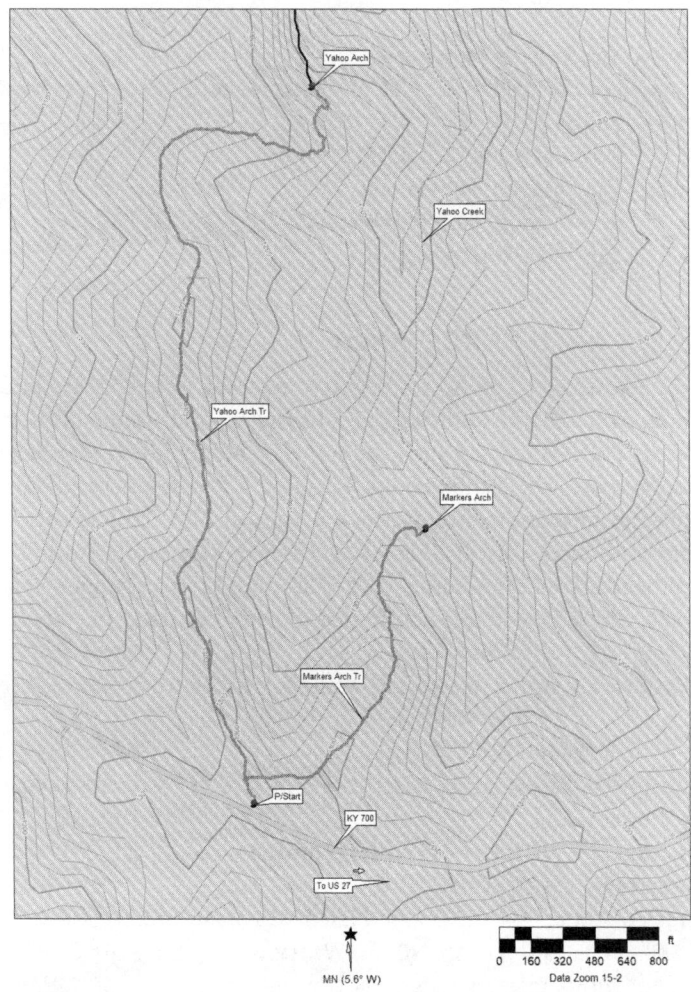

acclaimed that Kentucky has the most arches east of the Mississippi River, perhaps even the second most arches of any state outside of Utah.

The Daniel Boone National Forest is a geological wonderland. It has over 3,000 miles of clifflines, thousands of rock shelters and over 1,500 caves within its boundaries. This is all part of the Cumberland Plateau's sandstone cap eroding in various forms. Massive boulders can be found along streams and throughout the forest. All these clifflines lend themselves to waterfalls, also of which the Daniel Boone is rich. Rare flora and fauna call these caves and clifflines home, from the green salamanders

to the filmy fern to the Virginia big-eared bat. Many of the rock shelters were used by aboriginal Kentuckians as homes and part time hunt camps. Digging and camping in these rock shelters is illegal. Help preserve these sites for future national forest visitors.

The rock shelters around Yahoo Arch certainly seem possible candidates as archeological sites. Yahoo Arch is the centerpiece of a cliffline/rock shelter complex worth exploring. Markers Arch is smaller, but is arguably more dramatic as you come on it from above and see the length of the stone bridge from above. The surrounding cliffline is less impressive than Yahoo Arch but Markers Arch has an arch within the arch, as does Yahoo Arch.

The hike to these two stone spans is easy. Leave the trailhead on the Yahoo Arch Trail. Walk a little more than 100 feet then reach a trail intersection. Here, the Markers Arch Trail leaves right. Save it for later and keep straight on the Yahoo Arch Trail. Roll along the ridgetop in hickory, oak and beech. Pines and cedar find their place along the level easy trail. At .3 mile, the ridge narrows with a sparser tree cover. Be apprised this part of the path can grow brushy in summer.

At .7 mile, the trail curves easterly, dropping off the ridge. The hollow of Yahoo Creek lies below. A couple of quick switchbacks lead to steps carved from the exposed sandstone. The carved steps lead you down to the base of a cliffline. Come along a rockhouse then you turn the corner and at .9 mile are at Yahoo Arch and the rockhouse complex around it. The arch itself stands 17 feet high and is 70 feet long. The trail takes you directly beside a secondary, smaller window arch at the base of Yahoo Arch. Note the trees growing atop the deck of Yahoo Arch. The adjacent rockhouses are worth a look as well. The largest rockhouse is below Yahoo Arch. Like most stone spans in Kentucky Yahoo Arch can be difficult to photograph but is certainly worth a visit. The combination of the arch and nearby rockhouses renders the scene otherworldly.

To reach the second arch, backtrack on the Yahoo Arch Trail .9 mile nearly to the trailhead, then head east on the Markers Arch Trail. Briefly run parallel to KY 700 on a singletrack path among oaks, then gently turn northward in low slung brush. The Markers Arch Trail drops off the ridge into the head of the hollow of Yahoo Creek and at .4 mile Markers Arch appears before you. Spread 42 feet long this relatively narrow stone bridge allows a lot of light around it. Hikers walk directly under the arch. Note that Markers Arch also has an arch within an arch at its base. The cliffline and rockhouses around Markers Arch are much more modest than those around Yahoo Arch. From here it is a simple backtrack to the trailhead.

Mileages
0.0   Markers Arch Yahoo Arch trailhead
0.9   Yahoo Arch
1.8   East on Markers Arch Trail
2.2   Markers Arch
2.6   Markers Arch Yahoo Arch trailhead

LICK CREEK FALLS PRINCESS FALLS

Hike Summary: You will enjoy this there-and-back hike from the first step to the last. And you will take some interesting steps

Lick Creek Falls Princess Falls | 155

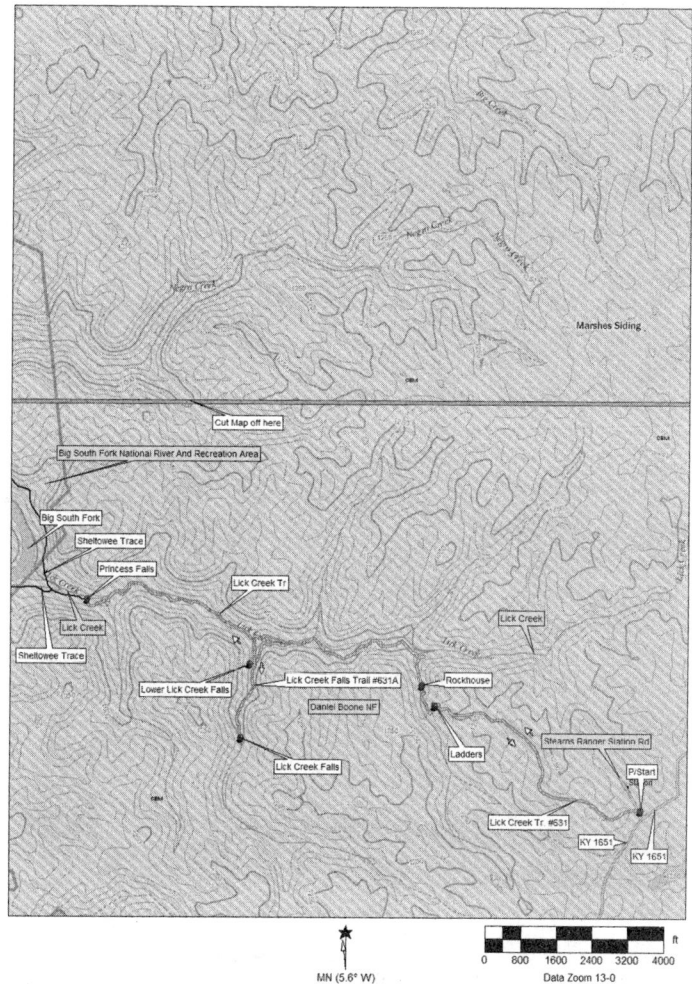

along the way—from metal ladders to stone stairwells through rock cathedrals to creek crossings to walks below clifflines. Those steps lead to 3 distinctly different waterfalls—Lick Creek Falls, Lower Lick Creek Falls and Princess Falls—that each make worthwhile destinations.

DISTANCE: 7.4-mile there-and-back with spur
HIKING TIME: 4.2 hours
DIFFICULTY: Moderate-difficult
HIGHLIGHTS: Lick Creek Falls, Lower Lick Creek Falls, Princess Falls, immense rockhouses

CAUTIONS: Some creek crossings
FEES/PERMITS: No fees or permits required
OTHER TRAIL USERS: None
TRAIL CONTACTS: Daniel Boone National Forest, Stearns Ranger District, 3320 US 27 North, Whitley City, KY 42653, (606)376-5323, www.fs.usda.gov/dbnf

Finding the trailhead: From traffic light #4 on US 27 at the intersection with KY 478 in Whitley City, head west on KY 478 for .1 mile, then turn left on KY 1651 south. Follow it for 1 mile to turn right onto Ranger Road. Follow Ranger Road just a short distance to reach a gravel parking area on your right, between two houses. GPS Trailhead Coordinates: N36° 42.899', W84° 28.857'

This waterfall-rich hike leaves from near Whitley City into the wild watershed of Lick Creek. First drop off a cliffline using metal ladders only to curve into a cool and immense rockhouse. From there dip into boulder-strewn Lick Creek. Next, enter a tributary to first find Lower Lick Creek Falls, then reach Lick Creek Falls. This 40-foot spiller dives from an overhanging rim into a prototypical eastern Kentucky sandstone rockhouse. Princess Falls is different yet again. Here, Lick Creek makes a right turn then makes a stream-wide 14-foot drop over a uniform ledge, gathering in a pool. Your return route takes you directly back up the Lick Creek valley.

Leave the parking area and look left for the trail sign and pole gate, where you walk along the edge of woods with a private house to your left. Join the Lick Creek Trail #631, a doubletrack path running along the Daniel Boone National Forest boundary. At .1 mile, stay right with the Lick Creek Trail, descending. Pass under a powerline at .3 mile. Ramble a ridgetop among hardwoods and some pines. At .9 miles, begin descending. At 1.2 miles, reach the first of two metal ladders (with handrails), allowing hikers to descend a pair of sheer clifflines.

Enter deeper into a tributary of Lick Creek, whereupon at 1.4 miles the trail curves under a huge rockhouse littered with big boulders and complemented by a delicate veil-like spill of water. Impressive stone steps curve behind the boulders and under the rockhouse, entering an otherworldly location of near pure rock, a significant singular highlight of the Daniel Boone National Forest.

Saddle alongside Lick Creek at 1.6 miles. Head downstream with the waterway flowing to your right. A mature forest rises above big boulders that litter the stream. At 2.3 miles, join the Lick Creek Falls Trail as it heads left. Turn up an unnamed tributary of Lick Creek, hiking a side slope well above the water. Reach another signed trail intersection at 2.5 miles. Here, stay left toward Lick Creek Falls. Just ahead you begin to hear Lower Lick Falls, a classic 16-foot cataract. However, you must scramble steeply downhill to your right to reach the spiller, noteworthy for the huge boulder astride the angled, widening froth of white that drops in two stages, collecting in a sandy, wood-scattered shallow pool.

After returning to the official trail, continue farther up the hollow on singletrack path bordered by clouds of rhododendron and mute mossy boulders. Curve under a wet overhanging cliffline then come to 40-foot Lick Creek Falls at 2.8 miles, located in the head of a grotto. Here, the tributary of Lick Creek recklessly plunges off a cleft in the cliff above, splattering onto a rocky basin, white noise echoing off the multihued rock enclosing Lick Creek Falls. You can walk behind the cataract, admiring it from multiple angles.

After lingering at this highlight, backtrack to the previous trail intersection, this time heading left. Quickly reach Lick Creek, rock hopping the waterway just upstream of a huge boulder then come to another trail intersection at 3.2 miles. Here, turn left, keeping downstream, back on the Lick Creek Trail #631. Look for a large, bluish pool below. Come to a trickier crossing at 3.7 miles. After making your way across Lick Creek continue down the left hand bank to reach a pair of crossings at 4.0 miles. However, another trail stays on the left hand bank and avoids these crossings. Take note if you do make these crossings that an illicit ATV trail comes in from the far bank hereabouts.

Just keep on the left hand bank of Lick Creek, quickly coming to a campsite and tributary stream entering from the left. Then reach Princess Falls at 4.1 miles. The cataract's location is somewhat unusual, located on a bend in Lick Creek. Here, after flowing over a wide rock slab the waterway makes its bend then executes its wider-than-high curtain-like nosedive into a generous plunge pool. The trail curves around and below the falls. A campsite lies below the cataract. This is a place to linger.

Your return trip is mostly backtracking, yet still avoiding the return spur trail up to Lick Creek Falls if you so choose. Just keep up the main Lick Creek valley the entire time, making it 3.3 miles back to the trailhead.

Mileages

0.0	Stearns Ranger Station Road trailhead
1.2	Descend a pair of metal ladders
1.4	Immense rockhouse
2.3	Left spur on Trail #631A to Lower Lick Creek Falls, Lick Creek Falls
2.5	Trail intersection, Lower Lick Creek Falls nearby
2.8	Lick Creek Falls, backtrack
3.1	Left at intersection, return toward Lick Creek Trail
3.2	Cross Lick Creek, left on Lick Creek Trail
3.7	Cross to left bank Lick Creek
4.0	Pair of quick crossings Lick Creek
4.1	Princess Falls, backtrack on Lick Creek Trail
5.0	Intersection, stay on left bank up Lick Creek
5.1	Intersection, backtrack up Lick Creek
7.4	Stearns Ranger Station Road trailhead

MARKS BRANCH FALLS GOBBLERS ARCH LOOP

Hike Summary: This highlight-rich valley-and-ridge circuit hike incorporates Kentucky's master path—the Sheltowee Trace—into the mix, taking you from a high and lonely land into a geologically astounding watershed whereupon Marks Branch Falls dives into a mighty rockhouse. From there, criss-cross Marks Branch, winding between boulders before returning to uplands, coming alongside a fortress-like rock wall. Breach the wall, pass a panoramic view then walk to (and through) Gobblers Arch before completing the circuit.

DISTANCE: 6.1-mile loop
HIKING TIME: 3.6 hours
DIFFICULTY: Moderate, does have 17 creek crossings
HIGHLIGHTS: Marks Branch Falls, Gobblers Arch, view, huge boulders
CAUTIONS: 17 creek crossings
FEES/PERMITS: No fees or permits required
OTHER TRAIL USERS: None
TRAIL CONTACTS: Daniel Boone National Forest, Stearns Ranger District, 3320 US 27 North, Whitley City, KY 42653, (606)376-5323, www.fs.usda.gov/dbnf

Finding the trailhead: From the intersection of US 27 and KY 92 just south of Whitley City, take KY 92 west for 6.5 miles to turn left on KY 1363, just after bridging the Big South Fork River at Yamacraw. Follow KY 1363 for 11 miles to a T-intersection and the end of the blacktop. Turn left on Bell Farm Road and follow it .1 mile, then turn right on Peters Mountain Road, Forest Road 139, and follow it 4.2 miles to the Peters Mountain trailhead, where parking is across the road in the Big South Fork National River and Recreation Area. Peters Mountain trailhead has a picnic table and restrooms. GPS Trailhead Coordinates: N36° 37.433', W84° 41.384'

Highlights are plentiful on this hike and the scenery between the highlights comprises some of the Bluegrass State's finest landscape. As with most part of the southern Daniel Boone National Forest, solitude is easy to find. Before your hike, do factor in the 17 crossings of Marks Branch. In winter and early spring expect to ford, but during summer and fall nimble hikers can make the crossings dry-shod.

Marks Branch Falls Gobblers Arch Loop

Leave the Peters Mountain trailhead and cross Divide Road to join the Sheltowee Trace southbound. Enter hickory-oak woodland on a single-track path. Pass a low cliffline while descending into a moister hollow with tulip trees and maples. Cross rhododendron-bordered Marks Branch at .5 mile. Lesser cascades drop below as you weave downstream through rhododendron, cutting deeper into a gorge.

At .7 mile, step over Marks Branch then circle above the stone amphitheater into which Marks Branch Falls makes its 80-foot dive. Rock ramparts rise all around as you curve into the stone echo chamber highlighted by the white ribbon of water splashing into a huge overhanging rockhouse, the walls of which are colored by the mixture of seeping water and minerals. A sand flat lies just beyond the cataract's base, along with fallen rocks and greenery. What a magnificent parcel of the Daniel Boone National Forest!

From Marks Branch Falls, the Sheltowee Trace takes you directly along Marks Branch. Begin a segment of repeatedly crisscrossing the waterway and sometimes walking straight down the stream, or finagling your way alongside the stream amid the rhododendron. Massive mossy boulders add geological wonder to the scene. Sometimes you will cross Marks Branch while twisting between these colossal rock pillars. At 1.2 miles, the stream itself flows under a house-sized boulder. All the while regal clifflines rise above the creek.

Pass the easily missed Marks Branch Trail leaving left at 1.6 miles. This intersection will occur when you are on the left bank of Marks Branch, heading downstream. The Marks Branch Trail allows a shortcut of the loop. The valley begins to widen beyond this trail intersection. Note the abundance of beech trees here. Pass a horse barrier just before reaching a trail intersection in the remains of a grassy field at 2.2 miles. To your right, a spur trail leads a quarter mile to Hemlock Grove Picnic Area, but does require a ford of Rock Creek.

Stay left with the Sheltowee Trace, reaching another trail intersection at 2.3 miles. Turn left here, joining the much less used Gobblers Arch Trail. The singletrack path immediately charges up a rising hardwood-clad ridgeline. Come alongside a cliffline and immense rock shelter at 2.7 miles. Continue cruising along some magnificent fortress like walls. Curve into a tributary of Marks Branch to climb past a low flow 15-foot waterfall at 3.0 miles. The Gobblers Arch Trail climbs out of the watershed into oak woods. Here, the path circles away from Marks Branch and into the piney clifftops above Rock Creek. Cruise the stone brow above Rock Creek to reach a spur trail at 3.7 miles. Here, a short path leads to an outcrop where panoramas open across and beyond the Rock Creek Valley.

Continue winding along the rim of the gorge then suddenly—out of nowhere at 4.3 miles—you are walking under Gobblers Arch! There is no way to miss it as the path leads you to and through the stone sight. Gobblers Arch measures 12 feet high and is 50 feet wide, formed through a rear collapse of a rock shelter. Enter the arch's low side then emerge at the larger more open side. The thick sturdy arch makes a dry refuge. From here the Gobblers Arch Trail climbs left then heads east in upland forest, joining an old doubletrack.

Emerge onto Forest Road 6102 at 4.7 miles. Follow the dead end gravel road south, passing the other end of the Marks Branch Trail at 5.1 miles. Stay with the forest road to meet Divide Road at 5.6 miles. Head left on Divide Road, skirting the boundary between the Daniel Boone National Forest to your left and Big South Fork National River and Recreation Area to your right. Soon find yourself back at the Peters Mountain trailhead at 6.1 miles, completing the hike.

Mileages
0.0 Peters Mountain trailhead
0.8 Marks Branch Falls
1.6 Marks Branch Trail
2.2 Spur to Hemlock Grove Picnic Area
2.3 Left on Gobblers Arch Trail
3.7 Rock Creek overlook
4.3 Gobblers Arch
4.7 FR 6102
5.1 Other end of Marks Branch Trail
5.6 Left on Divide Road
6.1 Peters Mountain trailhead

BUFFALO ARCH

Hike Summary: This hike takes place in the most southwesterly portion of the entire Daniel Boone National Forest. From this remote locale, join the Parkers Mountain Trail, tracing a ridge. Join the narrow Buffalo Arch Trail, circling the upper reaches of Right Fork Pennington Branch to reach secluded Buffalo Arch, just 1/10 mile from the Tennessee state line.

DISTANCE: 1.6-mile there-and-back
HIKING TIME: 0.9 hours
DIFFICULTY: Easy
HIGHLIGHTS: Natural arch, solitude
CAUTIONS: None
FEES/PERMITS: No fees or permits required
OTHER TRAIL USERS: None
TRAIL CONTACTS: Daniel Boone National Forest, Stearns Ranger District, 3320 US 27 North, Whitley City, KY 42653, (606)376-5323, www.fs.usda.gov/dbnf

SOUTHERN DANIEL BOONE NATIONAL FOREST

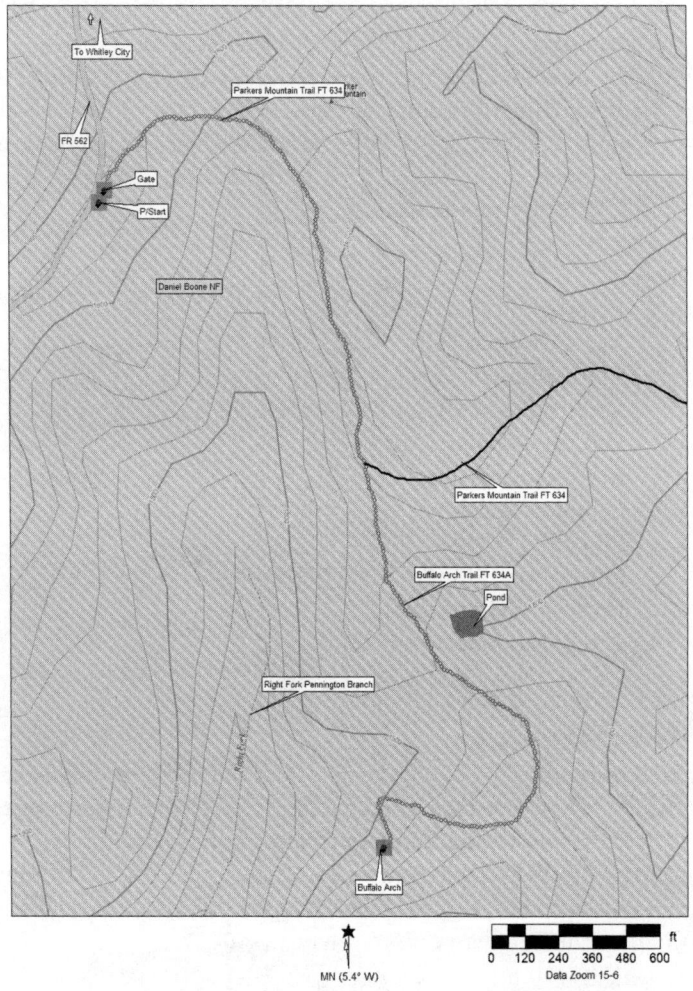

Finding the trailhead: From the intersection of US 27 and KY 92 just south of Whitley City, take KY 92 west for 6.5 miles to turn left on KY 1363, just after bridging the Big South Fork River. Follow KY 1363 for 11 miles to a T-intersection and the end of the blacktop. Turn right onto gravel Forest Road 564. Follow FR 564 for 1.2 miles then stay right with FR 564 as FR 137 goes left. Continue on FR 564 toward Parkers Mountain for 1.5 more miles to veer left onto FR 562. Stay with FR 562 for 5.8 miles then look left for a sign and small trailhead parking area as FR 562 curves

right. The parking area is small and limited. GPS Trailhead Coordinates: N36° 36.6310', W84° 45.9990'

Buffalo Arch is one of Daniel Boone National Forest least-visited trail-accessible arches. It is good piece from major roads to the arch. However, the drive to the trailhead courses through scenic and remote parcels of the DBNF as well as Big South Fork National River and Recreation Area. Furthermore, a fine and free national forest campground—Great Meadows—is located near Buffalo Arch and makes a fine base camp to explore the greater locale.

The walk to Buffalo Arch is easy, involving elevation changes of under 150 feet. This makes it good for families with young children or less able trail trekkers. Even though the trip to Buffalo Arch is not difficult, few hikers make their way here. If you desire additional trail mileage then tack on a walk along the Parkers Mountain Trail, part of which you follow en route to Buffalo Arch. The Parkers Mountain Trail leads 2 miles one-way to reach Rock Creek and Forest Road 137. Therefore, ambitious hikers can easily add 4 out-and back miles to the 1.6-mile Buffalo Arch endeavor.

The hike leaves the trailhead by passing around a pole gate on growing over trail-like Forest Road 6036. The Parkers Mountain Trail runs in conjunction with what is left of FR 6036 as it morphs from forest road to full-time path. Cruise the ridgetop in a mix of shortleaf pines, tulip trees and oaks with an understory of mountain laurel and greenbrier. Also, look for the horizontal limbs of black gum, whose leaves are among the earliest to display their autumn plumage. The walking is easy on the wide track. After 400 feet, the trail splits right as a faint logging track keeps left. Descend a bit as partial views open to the west into the Right Fork Pennington Branch valley below.

At .4 mile, reach an intersection. Here, the Parkers Mountain Trail leaves left 2 miles to Rock Creek at FR 137 while we veer right onto the more-heavily trod Buffalo Arch Trail. The woods thicken beside the level track. In winter you will more easily see the pond on trail left at .5 mile. At .6 mile the Buffalo Arch Trail narrows to become a singletrack pure footpath. Umbrella magnolias rise overhead. Their 18-24 inch lobed leaf and circular leaf growth pattern make it easy to identify. Umbrella magnolias trees grow in the moist drainages of the Daniel Boone. Unlike the more commonly known Southern magnolia, umbrella magnolias lose their leaves each year. They both produce copious, fragrant blooms. The white flowers of the umbrella magnolia range from 7 to 10 inches in size, and stand out in a springtime forest. Umbrella magnolia grows throughout eastern Kentucky as well as southern West Virginia and Tennessee's Cumberland Plateau, though it sporadically stretches westerly to the Ozarks, northeasterly into Pennsylvania and southeasterly to the coastal Carolinas.

Spot clifflines to your left before crossing a streambed around which rise a profusion of ferns and rhododendron. Once across the streambed step forth to the geological wonderment that is Buffalo Arch. Legend tells that aboriginal Kentuckians stood atop Buffalo Arch to gain an advantage while hunting the shaggy bison.

Buffalo Arch extends outward from the cliffline to your left. The wide, flattish arc curvature stands 18 feet 6 inches above the ground at its tallest then slopes rightward to the ground. The stone span is 81 feet

8 inches long. A dry shelter, Buffalo Arch was likely used for more than a hunting perch, providing a dry, sandy refuge from the elements, too. Today, the wide geological feature is one of the least visited arches in the Daniel Boone National Forest, providing solitude for those who make their way to it. Enjoy your time here, shooting pictures and admiring Buffalo Arch from multiple angles.

Mileages
- 0.0   Parking area on FR 562
- 0.4   Parkers Mountain Trail leaves left
- 0.8   Buffalo Arch
- 1.6   Parking area on FR 562